JOURNEY TO THE SACRED GARDEN

JOURNEY TO THE SACRED GARDEN

Published in the United States by When Heaven Speaks, LLC
P.O. Box 55
Pooler, GA 31322
www.whenheavenspeakspublishing.com

Copyright © 2020 TWYLIA G. REID
ISBN: 9798578672972

All rights reserved. No part of this book may be reproduced, distributed, or transmitted in any form by any means, graphic, electronic, or mechanical, including photocopy, recording, taping, or by any information storage or retrieval system, without permission in writing from the publisher, except in the case of reprints in the context of reviews, quotes, or references.

Special discounts are available on bulk quantity purchases by book clubs, associations, and special interest groups. For details, email: info@twyliareid.com or call 912-335-3799.

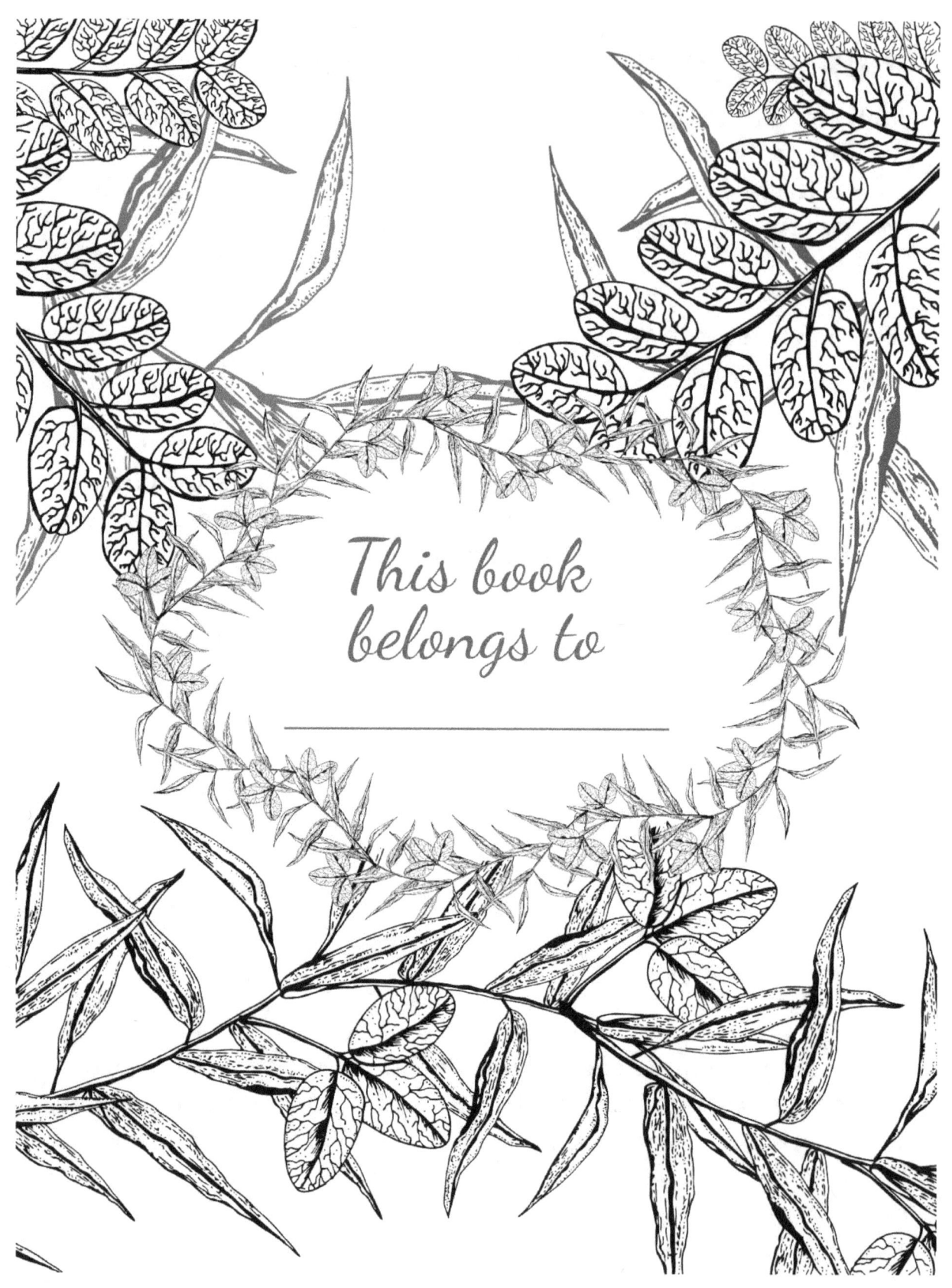

SACRED GARDENS

God is the Master Designer, not only of you and me, and of the world in which we live but also of the first garden! "The LORD God planted a garden eastward in Eden, and there He put the man whom He had formed. And out of the ground the LORD God made every tree grow that is pleasant to the sight and good for food. The Tree of Life was also in the midst of the Garden, and the tree of the Knowledge of Good and Evil. Now a river went out of Eden to water the garden." Genesis 2:8-10 (NKJV)

Many of you may have heard the phrase "Life began in the Garden". After God finished creating the universe, the sky, the stars, the land, and the sea, as well as all the creatures within it, He created man. And, the LORD God placed him in the Garden and asked him to tend it. The first garden, the first gardener, and the beginning of the first occupation of Mankind was gardening!

Gardens of the Bible were places of beauty, shelter, and sustenance. The fruit trees and vines, fragrant herbs and other useful plants, as well as natural water supplies, were all key elements of design. God created the first garden, Eden. After Eden, the Bible mentions numerous gardens and their qualities. In the Song of Solomon 6:11 and Luke 13:19, a garden is referred to as a place of shelter and shade, and also as a place of protection Song of Solomon 4:12.

The garden mentioned in Esther 1:5 was the setting for a dazzling social event when King Ahasuerus hosts a 7-day feast. It is also recognized as a place of provision of food in Jeremiah 29:5,28 as well as Amos 9:14. Gardens of the Bible are also seen as a place for quiet retreat and meditation. A second Garden of Eden is foretold in Revelation 22:2. At the end of time, as we know it, there will be a New Heaven and a New Earth (Revelation 21:1), and a New Jerusalem. The New Jerusalem is to be planted with the Tree of Life. The trees planted on either side of the river that runs through the city will bear twelve fruits, each yielding its fruit every month, as well as leaves for the healing of the nations!

Now you can unearth artistic annuals and bountiful blooms in this ready-to-color collection. Isn't it amazing that coloring books are not just for children? Adult coloring books are a great way for grown-ups to express their inner artist and relieve stress. "Adult coloring books are great for a mindful activity, meaning they help you focus in the moment, mindfully," says Cara Maksimow, a therapist in private practice in Chatham, New Jersey. Unleash your hidden creative potential with each one-of-a-kind masterpiece, from quality realistic looking flowers to flowers filled with remarkable patterns. Many psychologists, researchers, and therapists actually prescribe adult coloring books to patients as an alternative to traditional medicine. Whether you use colored pencils to create your own drawings or doodle in an adult coloring book, your mind and body relax when you are engaging in a focused, soothing activity.

Adult coloring books are usually geared towards relieving stress because they have intricate designs that challenge the fine motor skills and attention span of even the most detail-oriented adults. According to a 2015 study published in the journal Frontiers in Psychology, cool colors like blue and green can induce calm, while hot colors like red and orange can be energizing and stimulating.

These coloring books can relieve stress similarly to the way that meditation can reduce stress levels. Combining coloring into your daily routines may help you feel distracted in a good way, with less stress and anxiety. Therefore, allowing your creative juices to flow freely. Decision fatigue can be an awful thing to deal with each day. Fortunately, coloring limits this to only two decisions...which page and which color! Coloring can add meaning to life and make you feel like a kid again. No matter how old you are it's always a great feeling engaging in activities that force your youthful side to reappear. How awesome is that? So, let's start coloring to boost your well-being and mood.

Welcome to the sacred gardens!

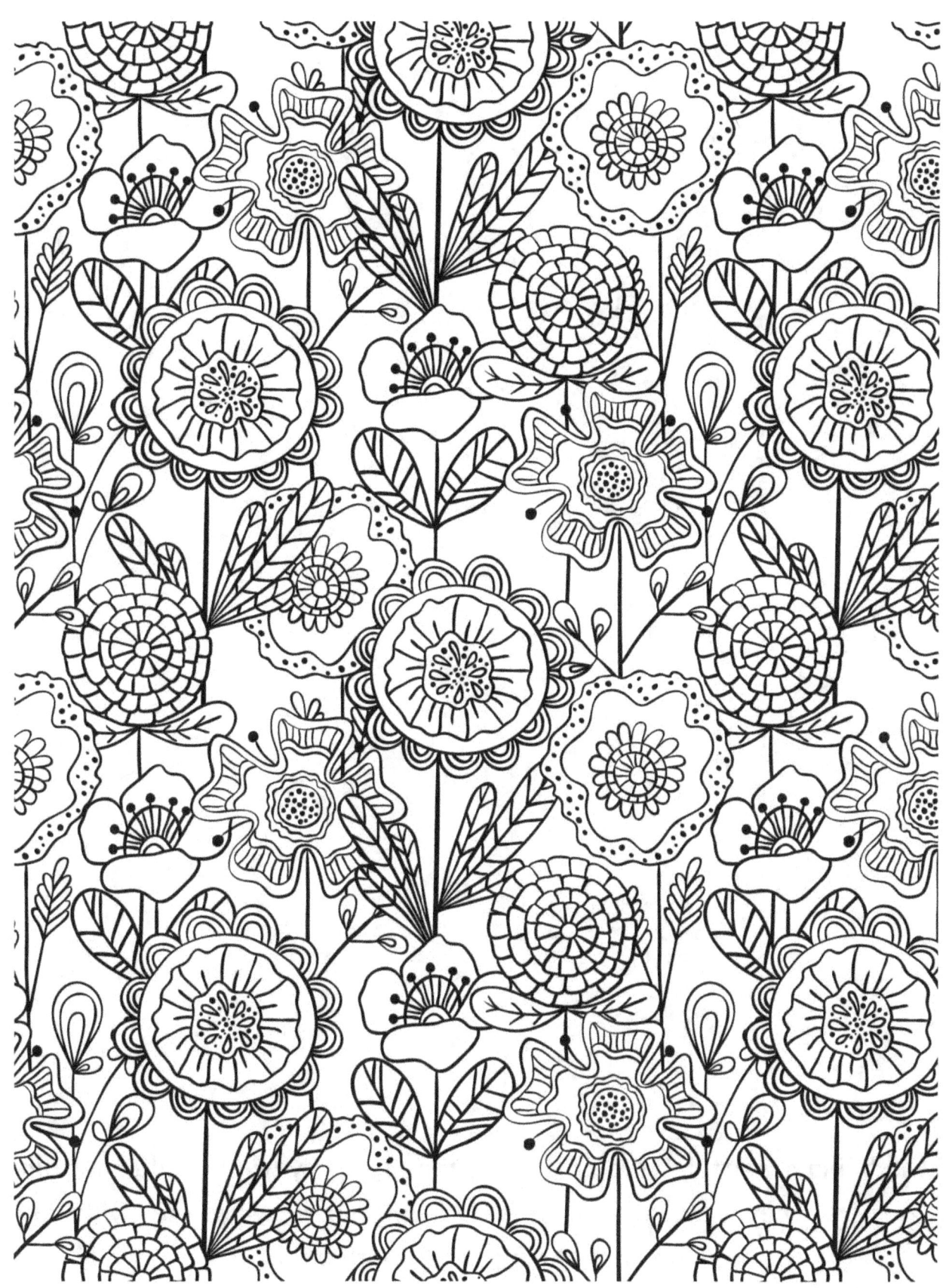

"And I will bring my people Israel back from exile. They will rebuild the ruined cities and live in them. They will plant vineyards and drink their wine; they will make gardens and eat their fruit." (Amos 9:14)

"The land you are entering to take over is not like the land of Egypt, from which you have come, where you planted your seed and irrigated it by foot as in a vegetable garden." (Deuteronomy 11:10)

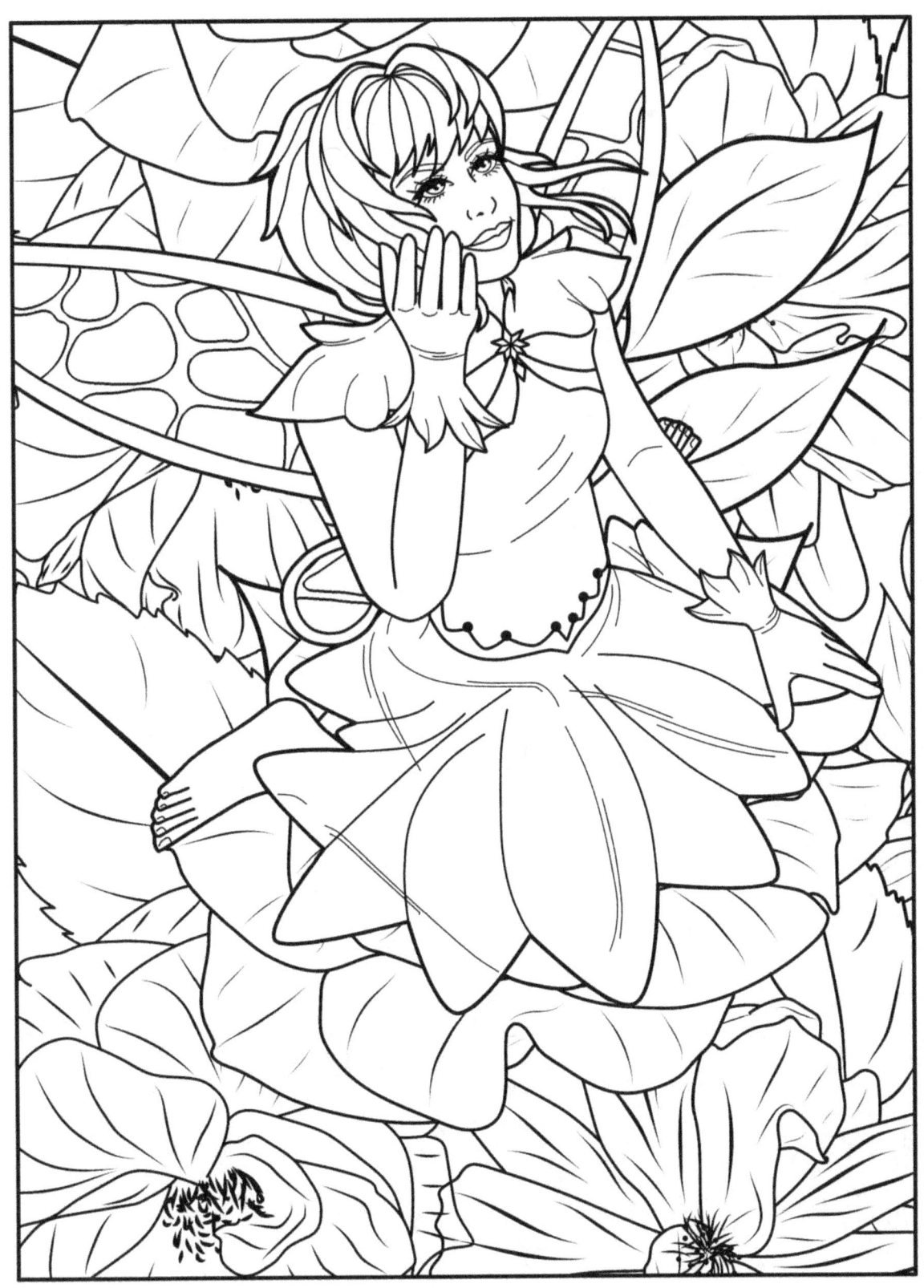

"I made gardens and parks and planted all kinds of fruit trees in them." (Ecclesiastes 2:5)

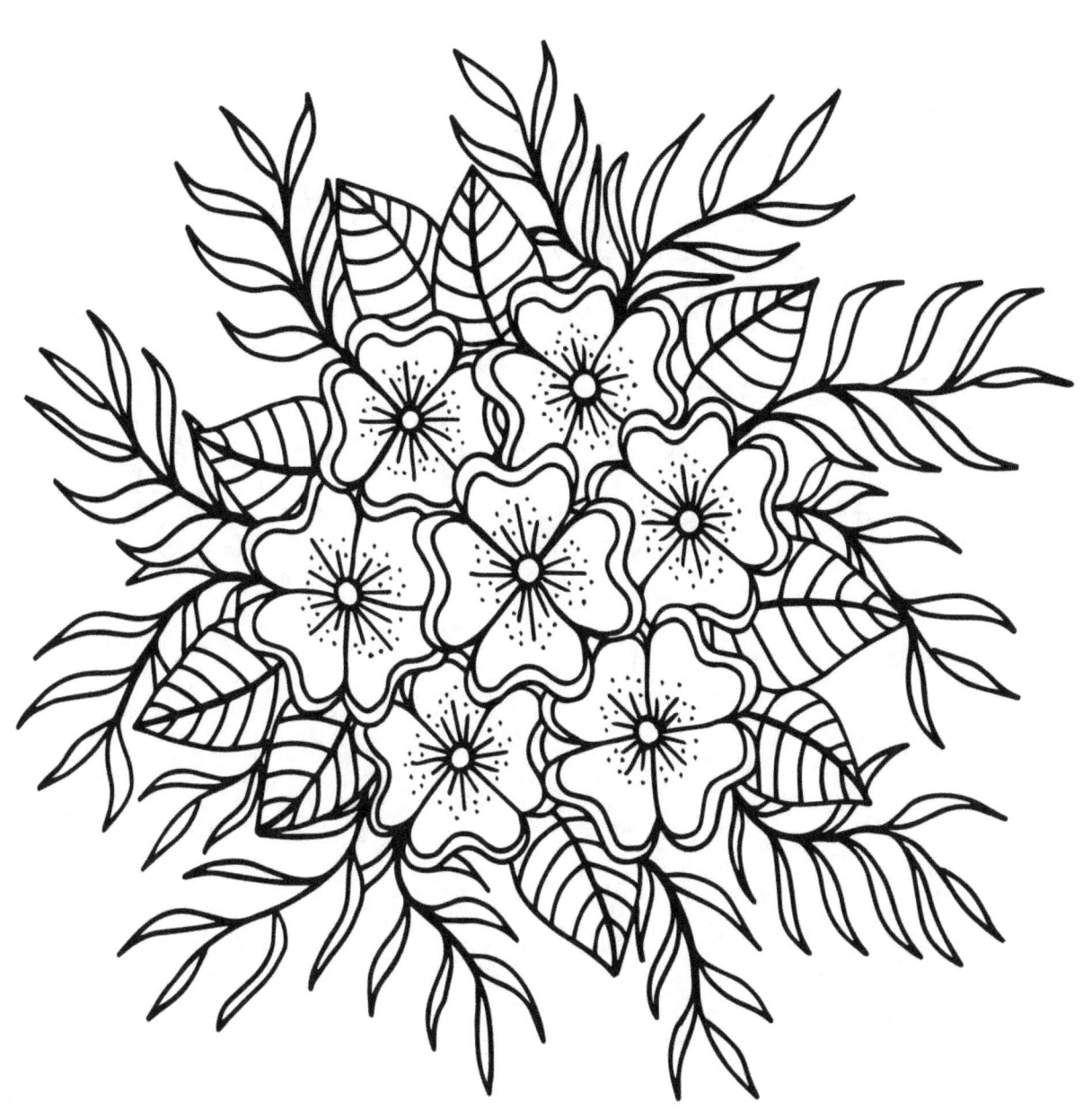

"Now the LORD God had planted a garden in the east, in Eden; and there he put the man he had formed." (Genesis 2:8)

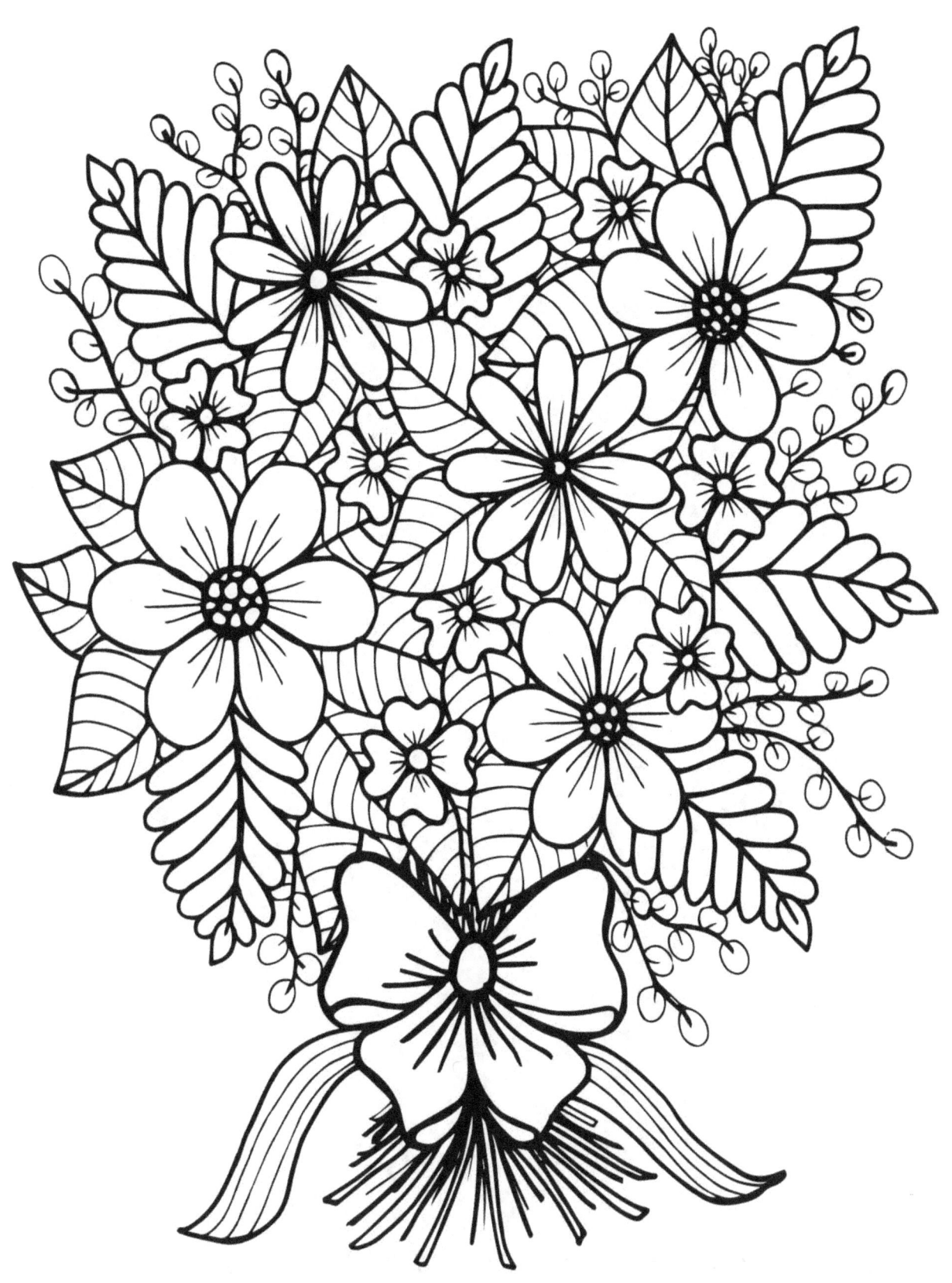

"The LORD will surely comfort Zion and will look with compassion on all her ruins; he will make her deserts like Eden, her wastelands like the garden of the LORD. Joy and gladness will be found in her, thanksgiving and the sound of singing." (Isaiah 51:3)

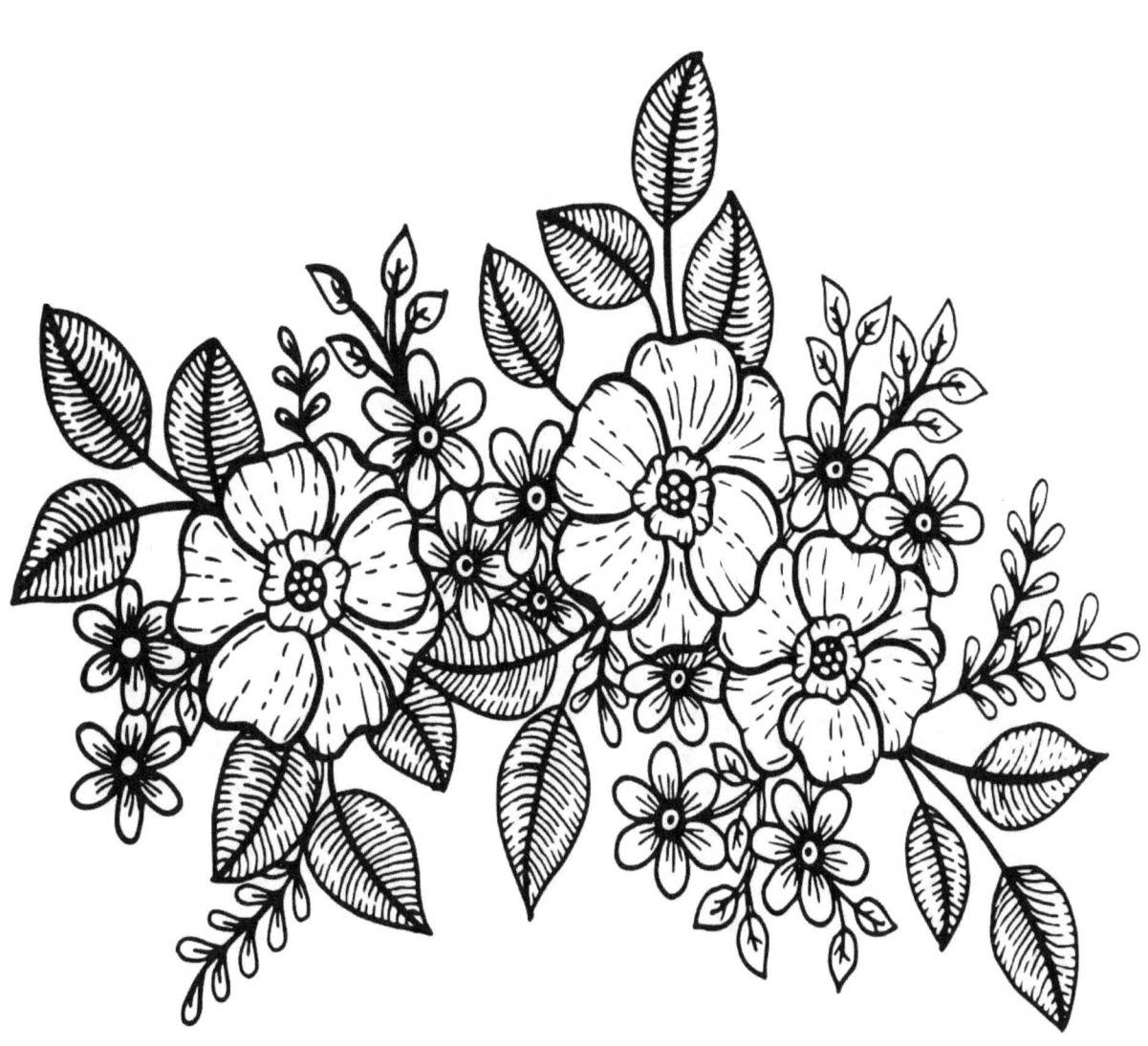

"The LORD will guide you always; he will satisfy your needs in a sun-scorched land and will strengthen your frame. You will be like a well-watered garden, like a spring whose waters never fail." (Isaiah 58:11)

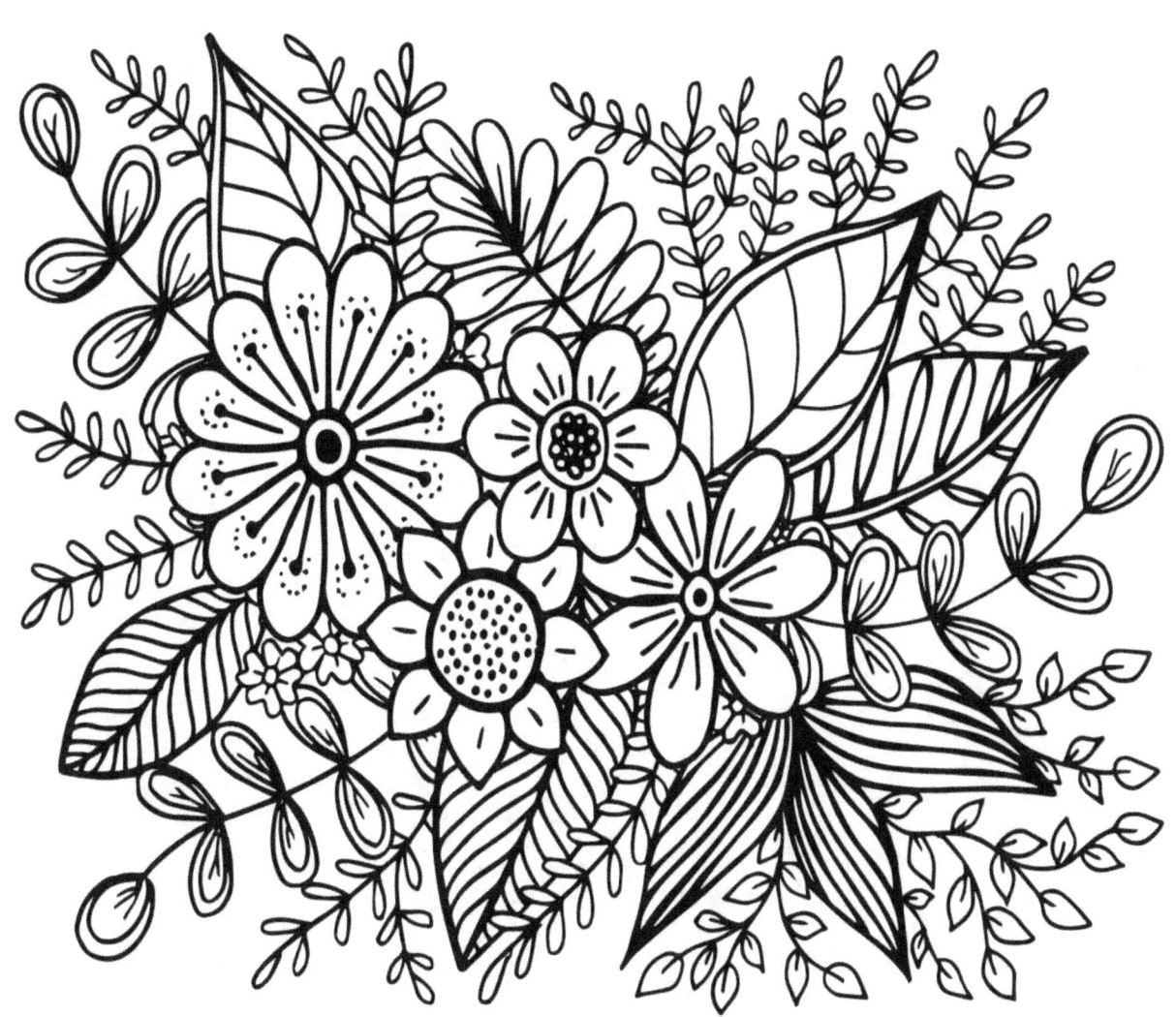

"For as the soil makes the sprout come up and a garden causes seeds to grow, so the Sovereign LORD will make righteousness and praise spring up before all nations."
(Isaiah 61:11)

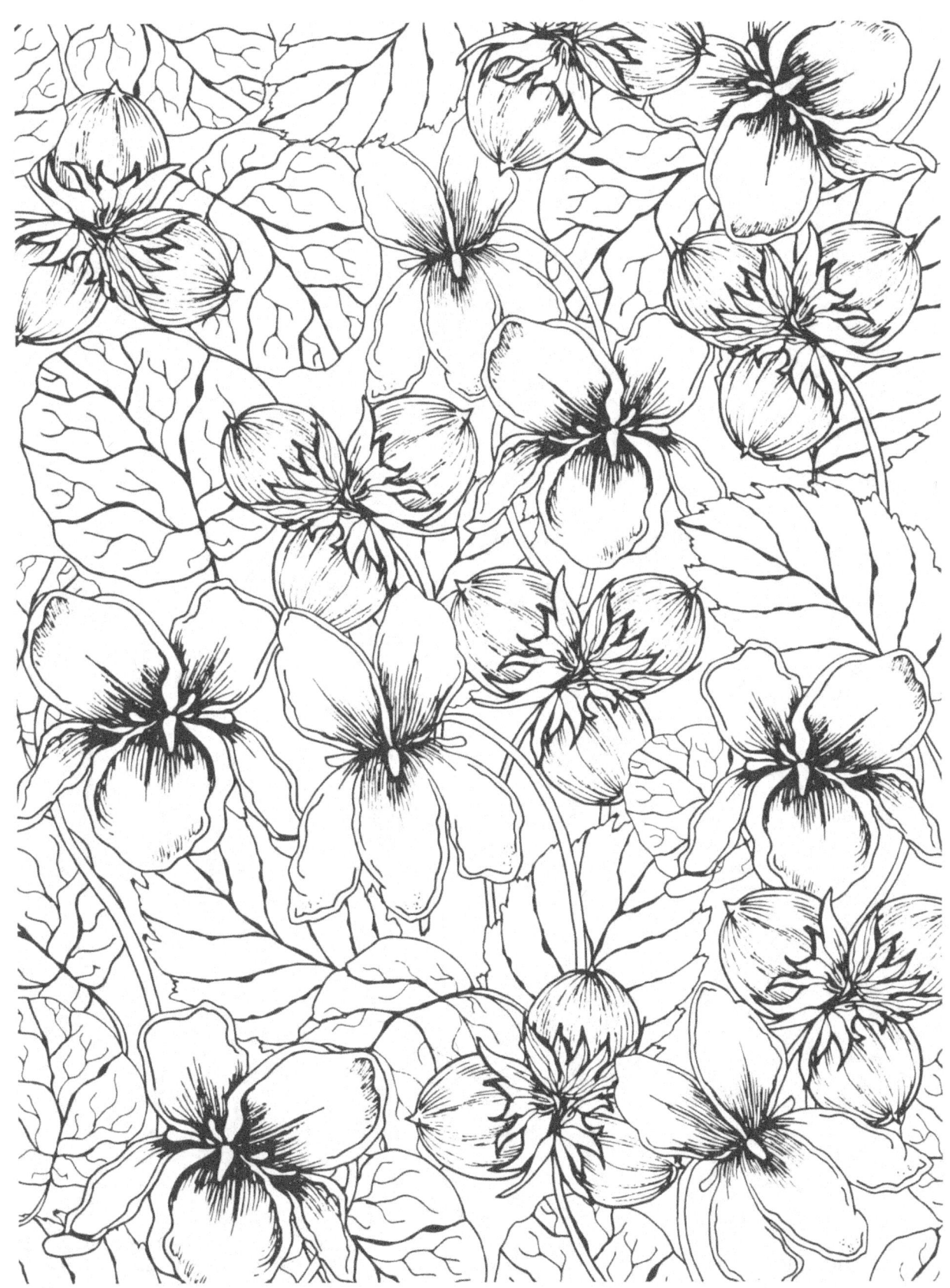

"They will build houses and dwell in them; they will plant vineyards and eat their fruit." (Isaiah 65:21)

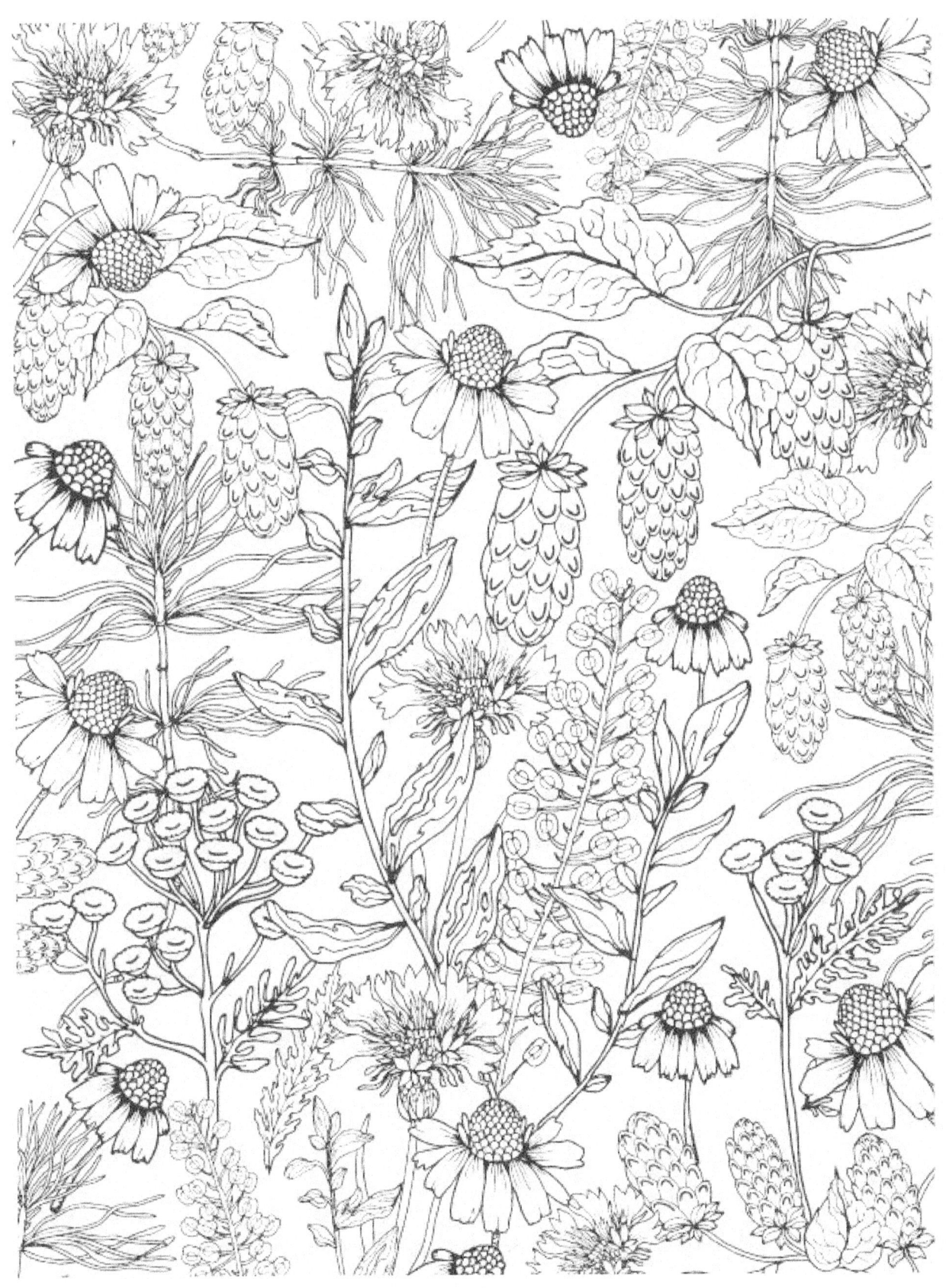

"Build houses and settle down; plant gardens and eat what they produce." (Jeremiah 29:5)

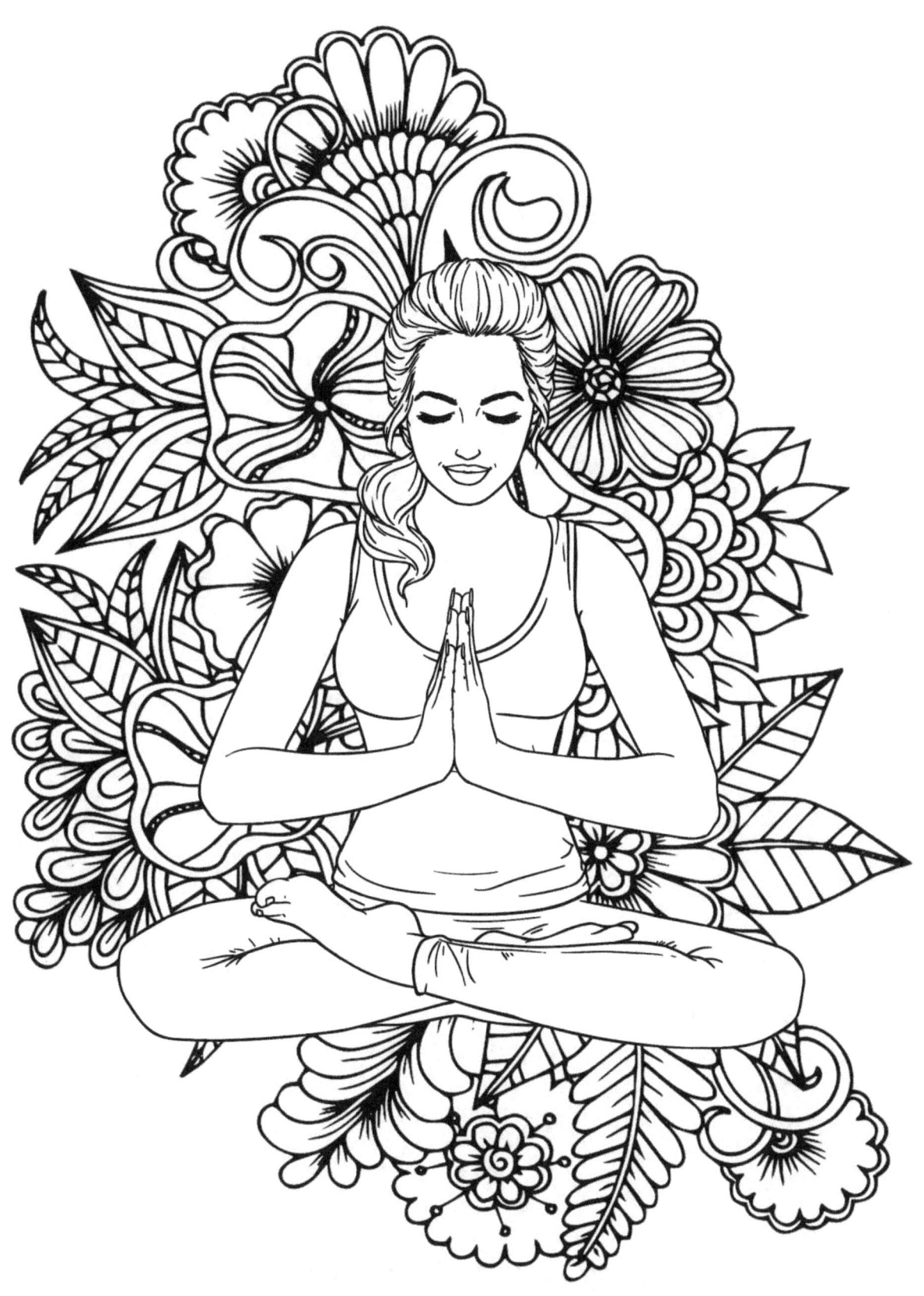

"It is like a mustard seed, which a man took and planted in his garden. It grew and became a tree, and the birds perched in its branches." (Luke 13:19)

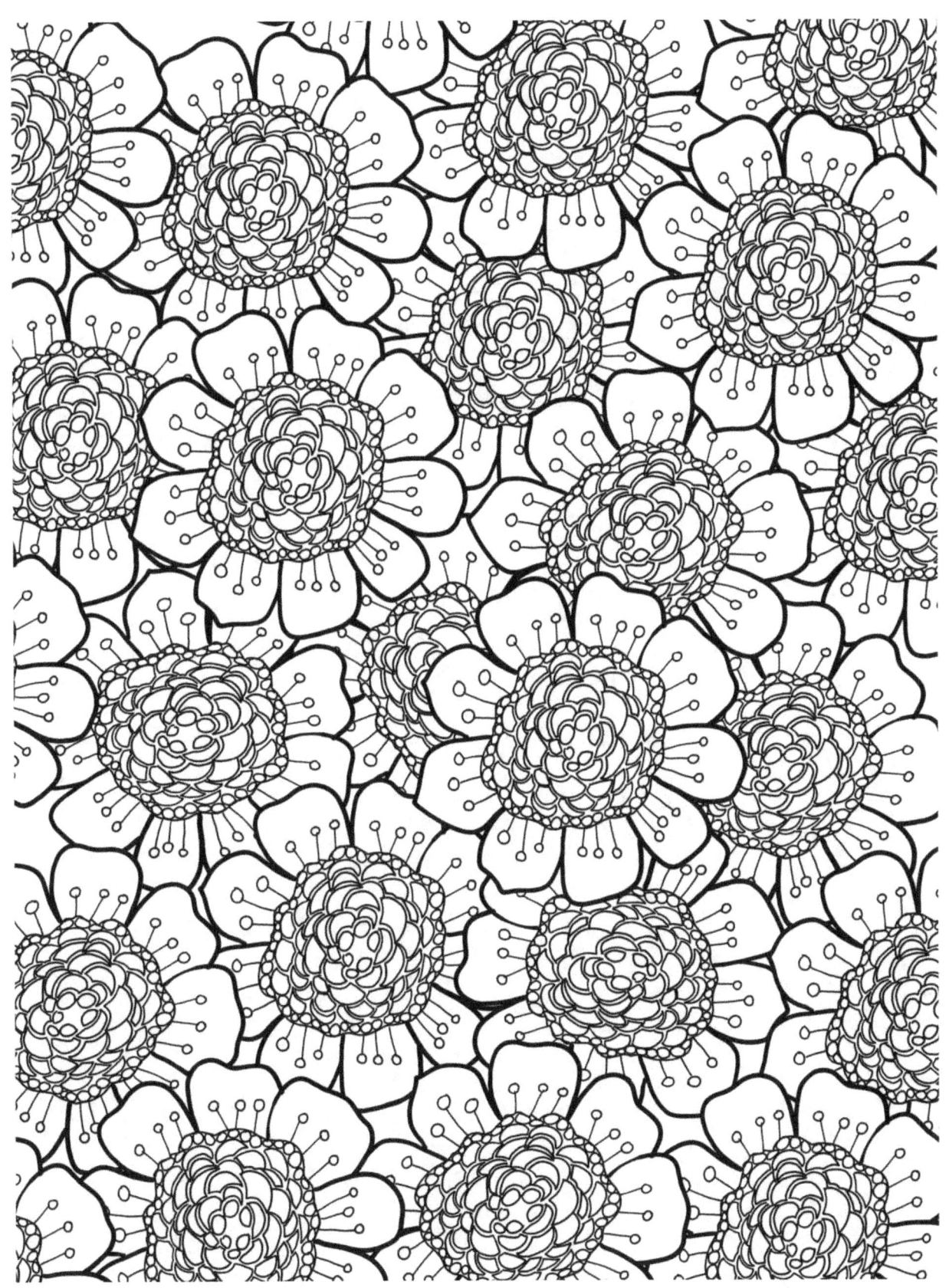

"Draw close to God and He will draw close to you." (James 4:8)

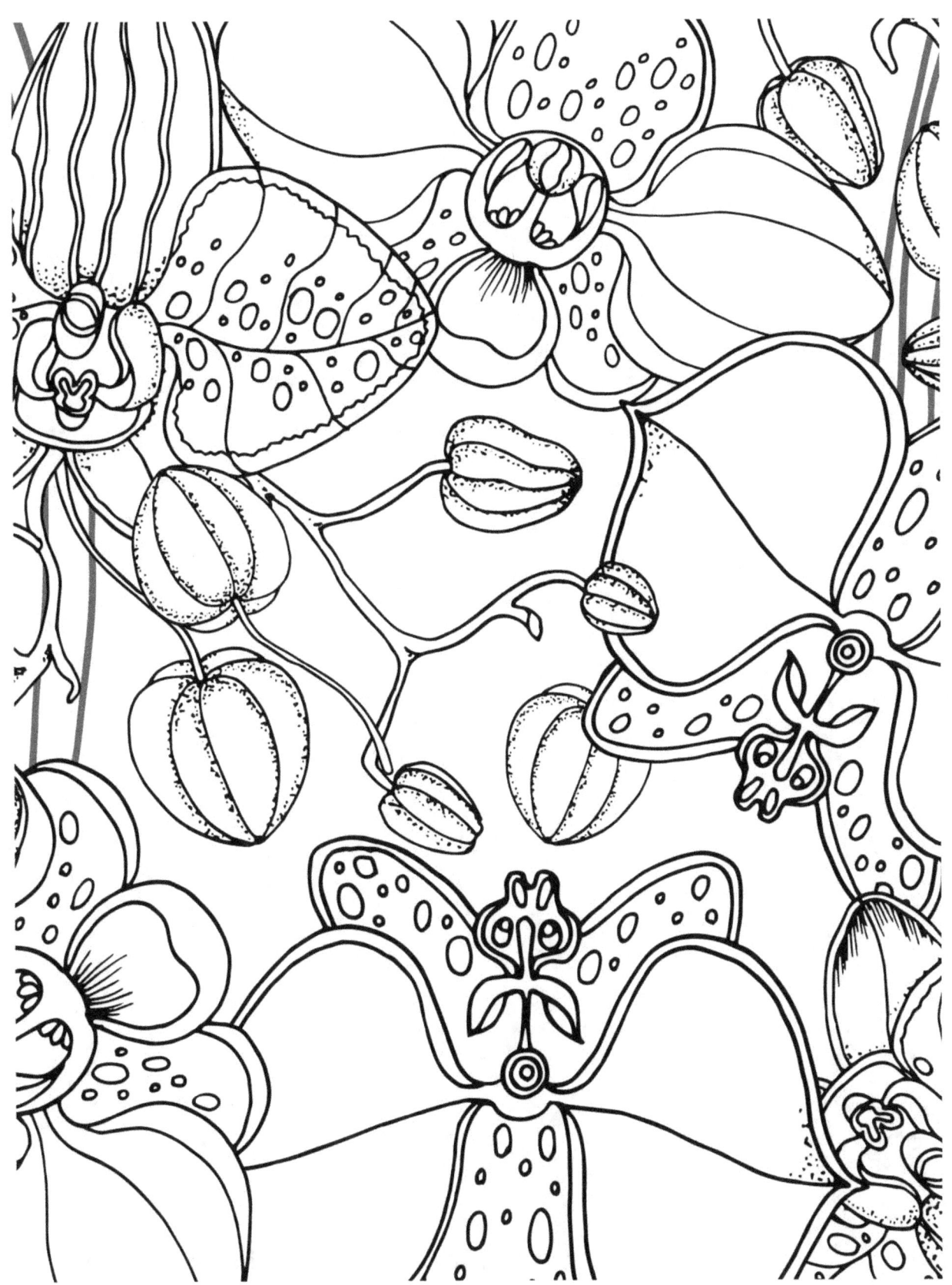

"Like valleys they spread out, like gardens beside a river, like aloes planted by the LORD, like cedars beside the waters." (Numbers 24:6)

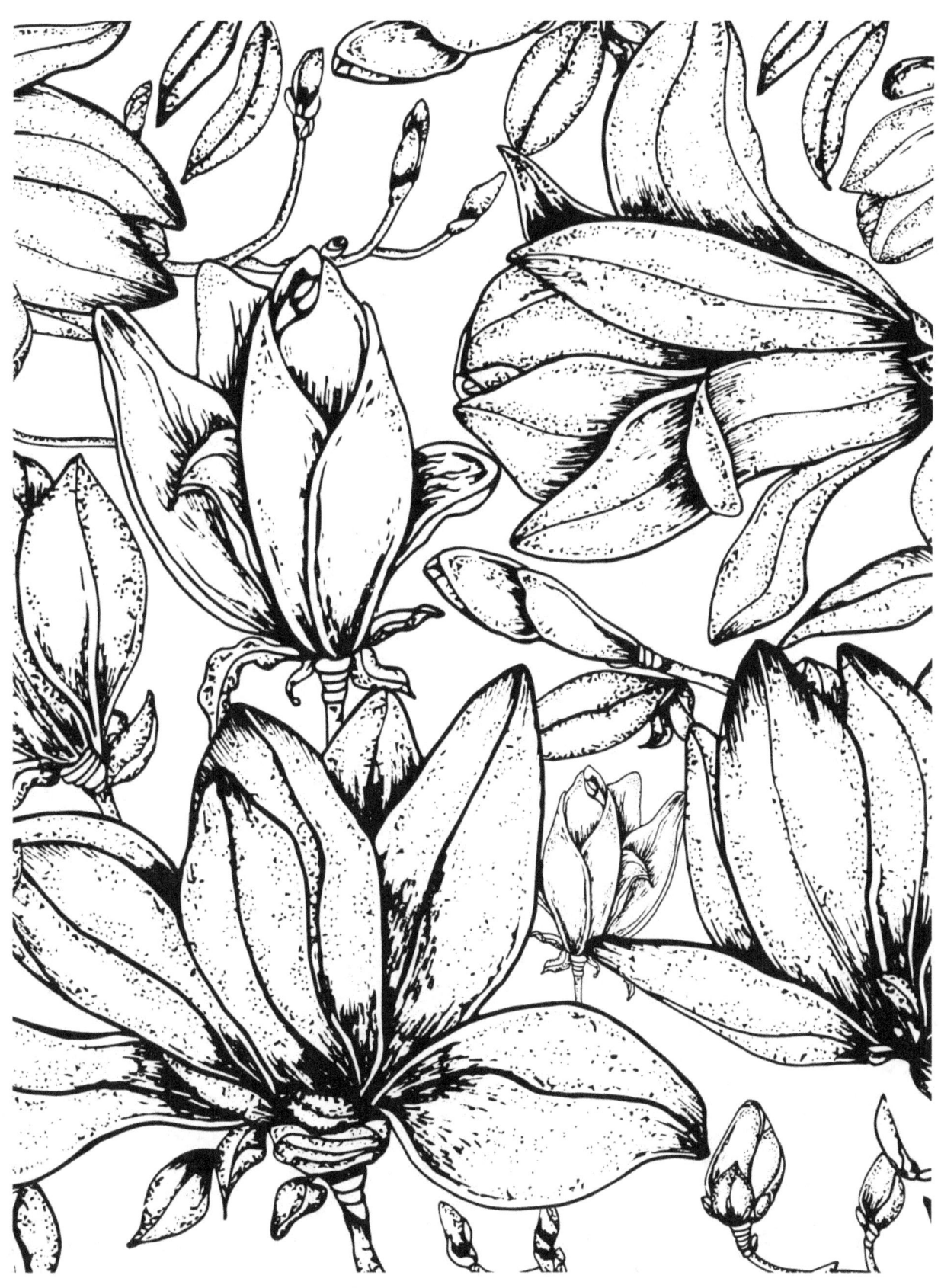

"You are a garden fountain, a well of flowing water streaming down from Lebanon."
(Song of Songs 4:15)

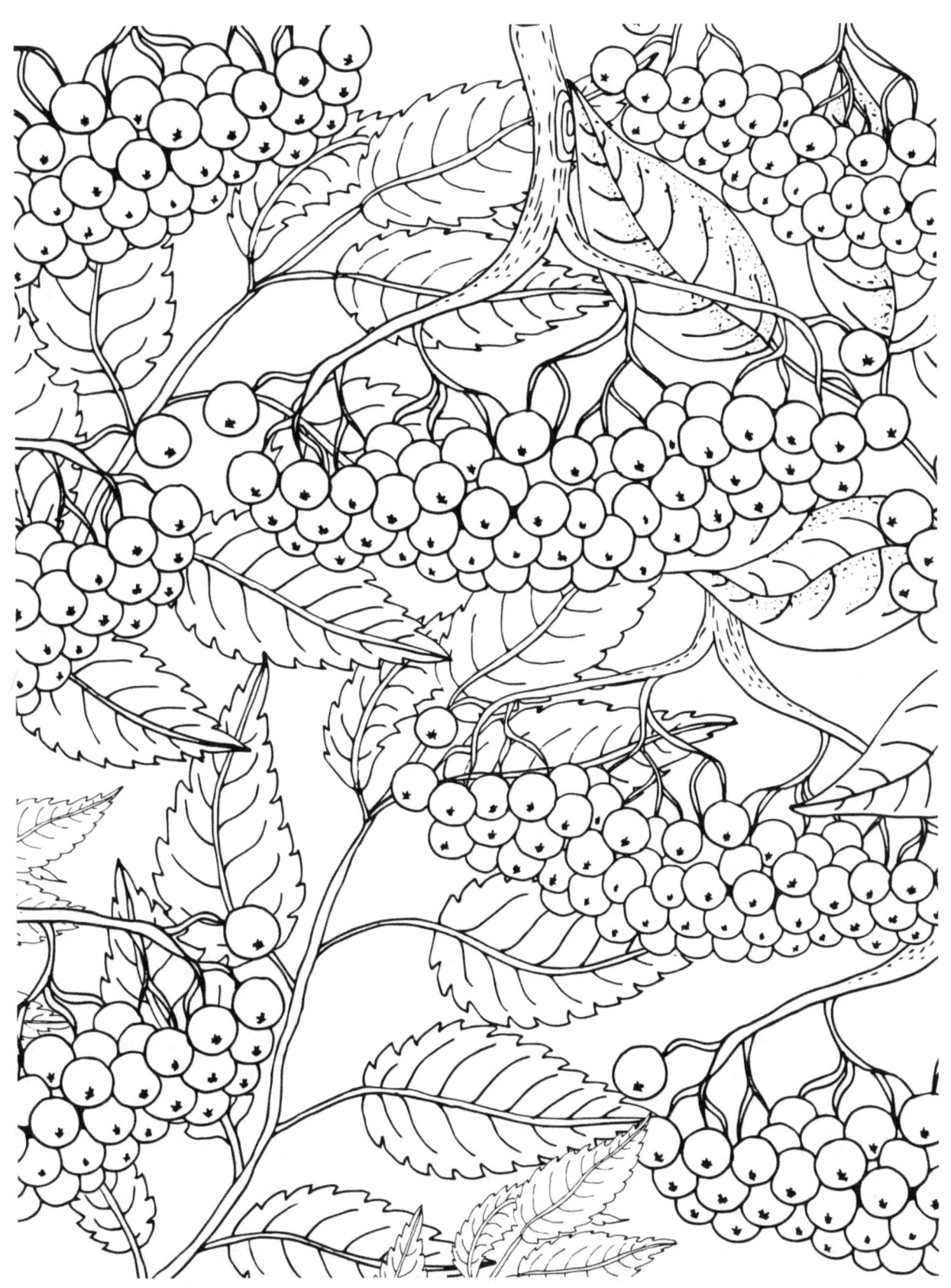

"I have come into my garden, my sister, my bride; I have gathered my myrrh with my spice. I have eaten my honeycomb and my honey; I have drunk my wine and my milk. Eat, friends, and drink; drink your fill of love." (Song of Songs 5:1)

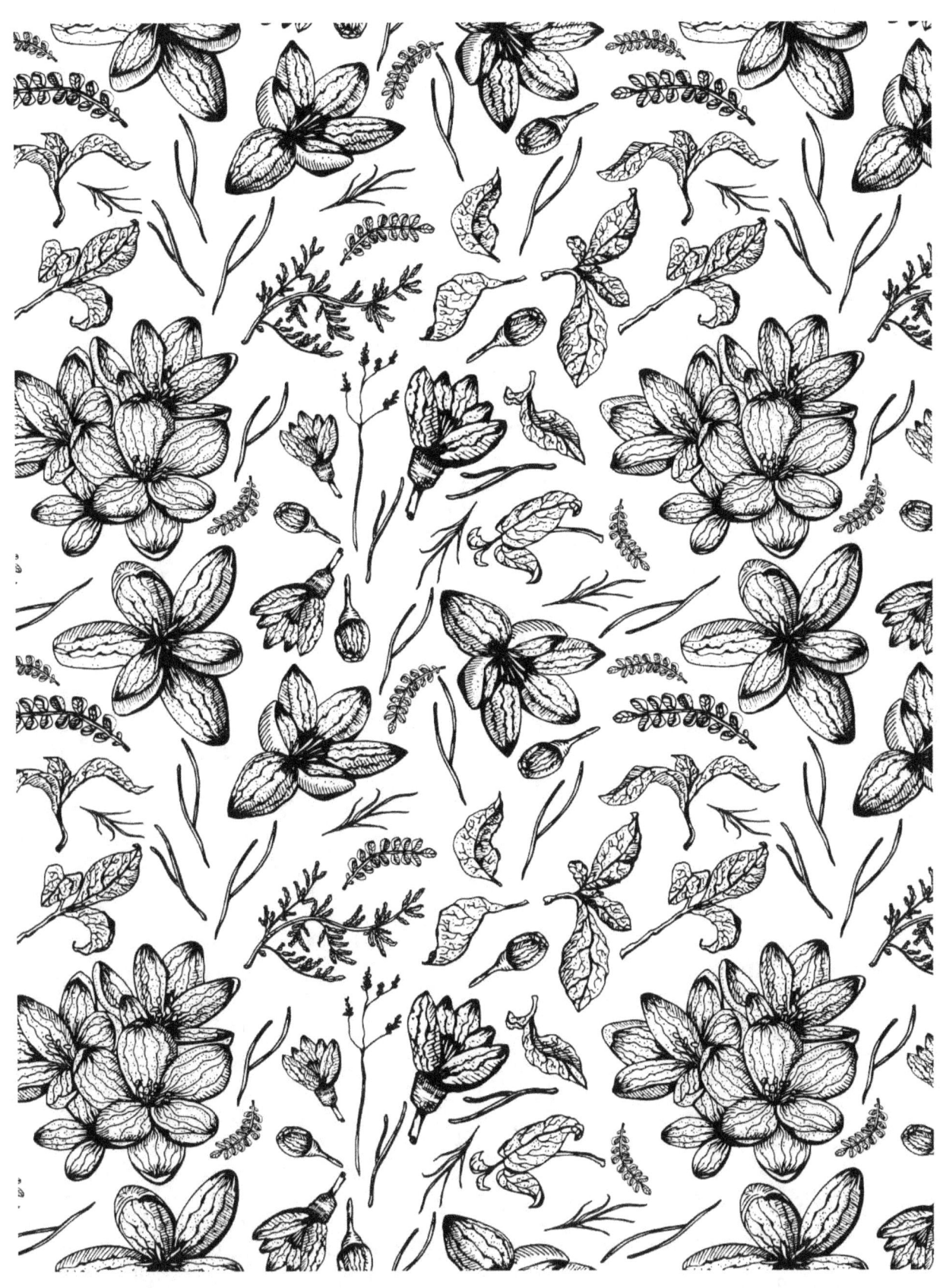

"Every branch in me that does not bear fruit he takes away, and every branch that does bear fruit he prunes, that it may bear more fruit." (John 15:2)

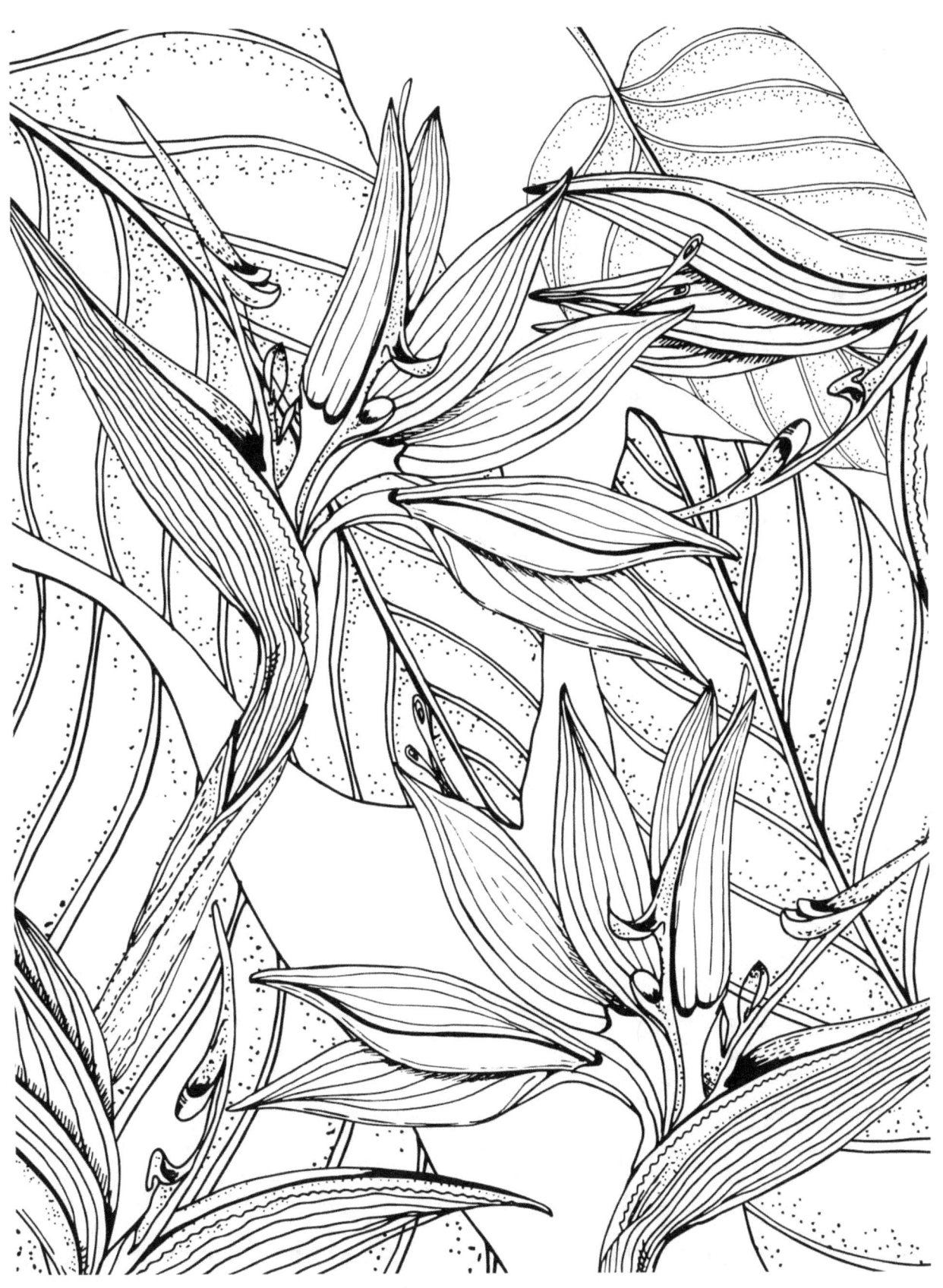

"He answered, "Every plant that my heavenly Father has not planted will be rooted up." (Matthew 15:13)

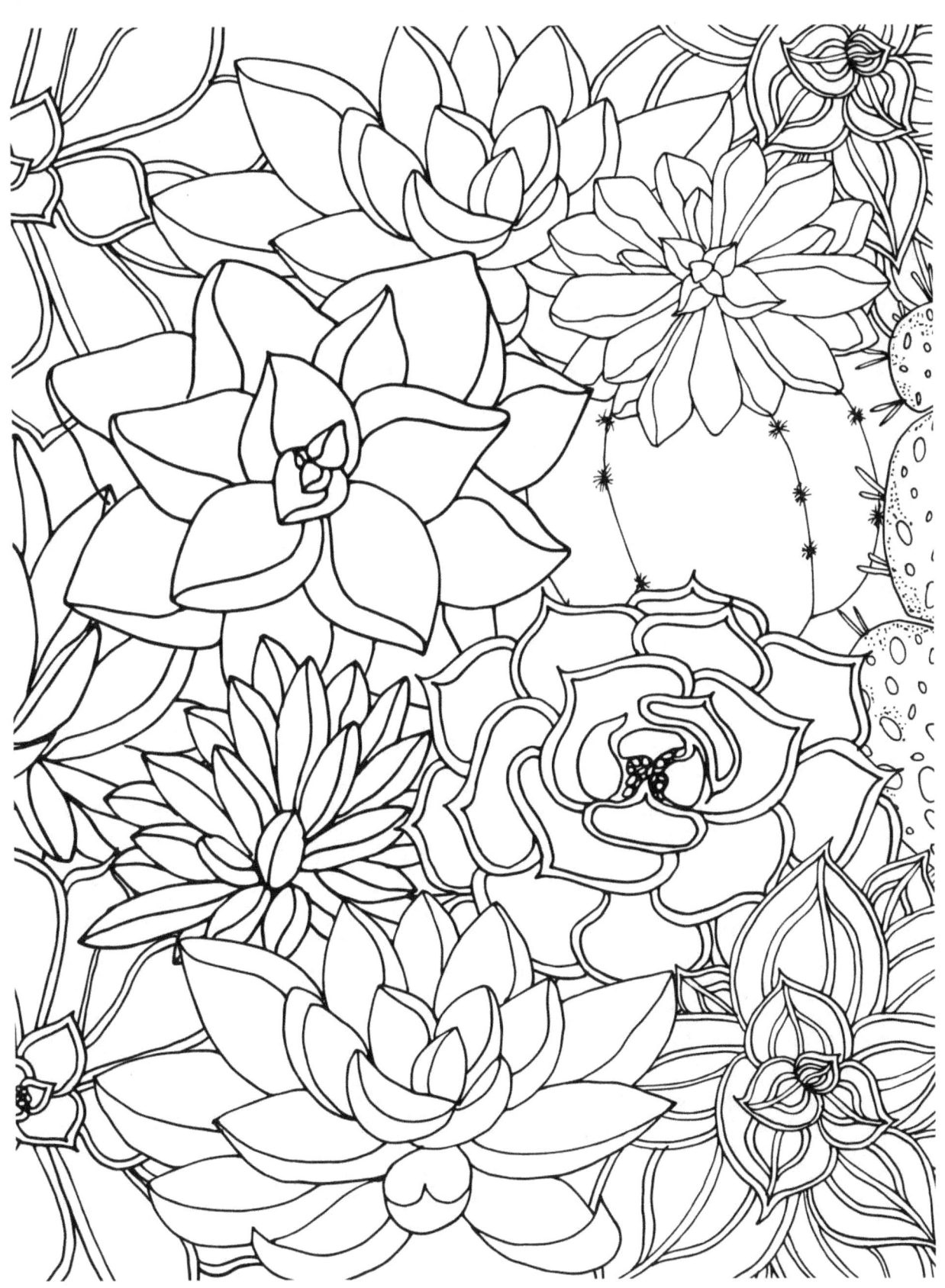

"I am the true vine, and my Father is the vinedresser." (John 15:1)

"The grass withers, the flower fades, but the word of our God will stand forever."
(Isaiah 40:8)

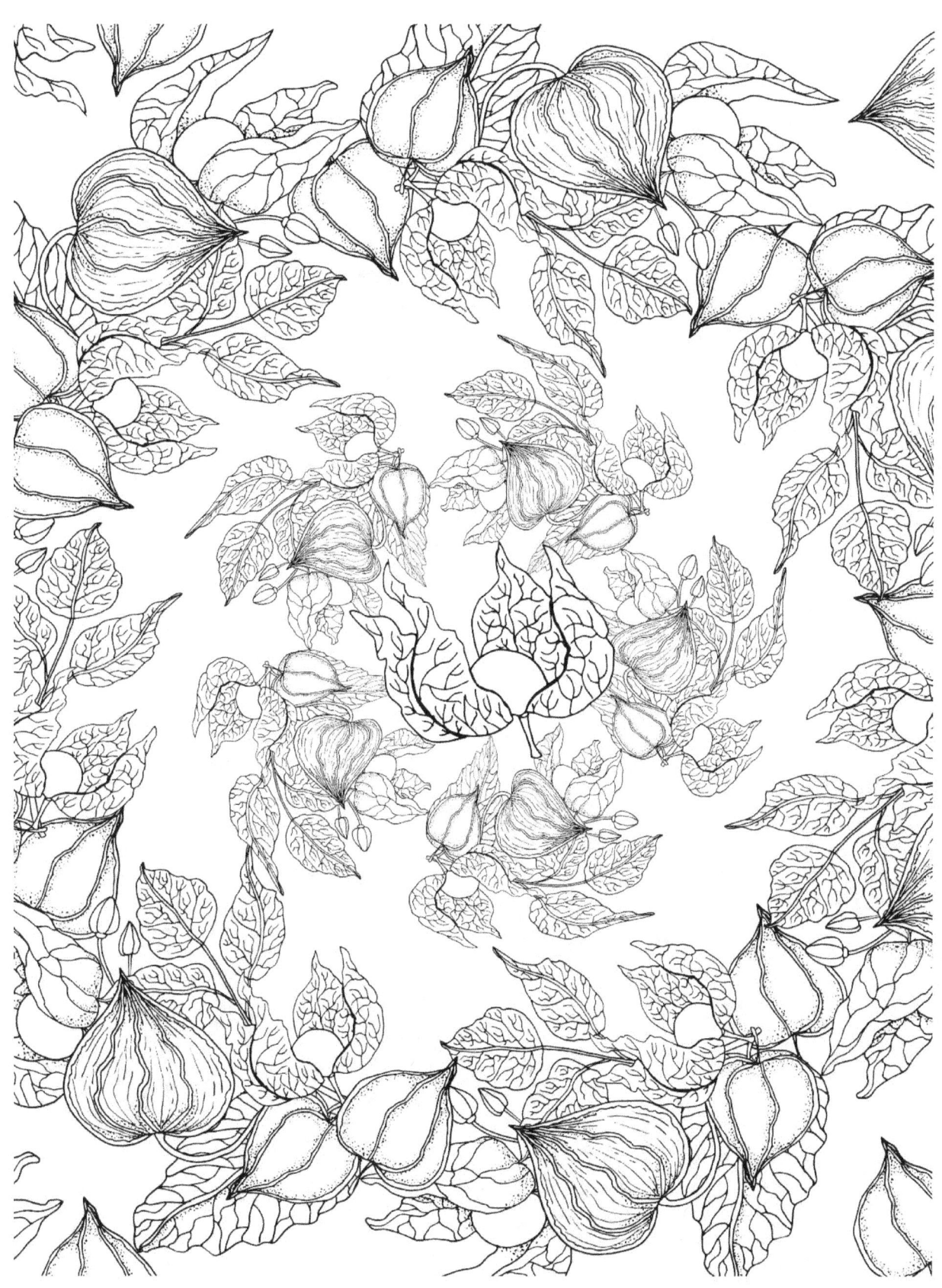

"I am a rose of Sharon, a lily of the valleys." (Song of Solomon 2:1)

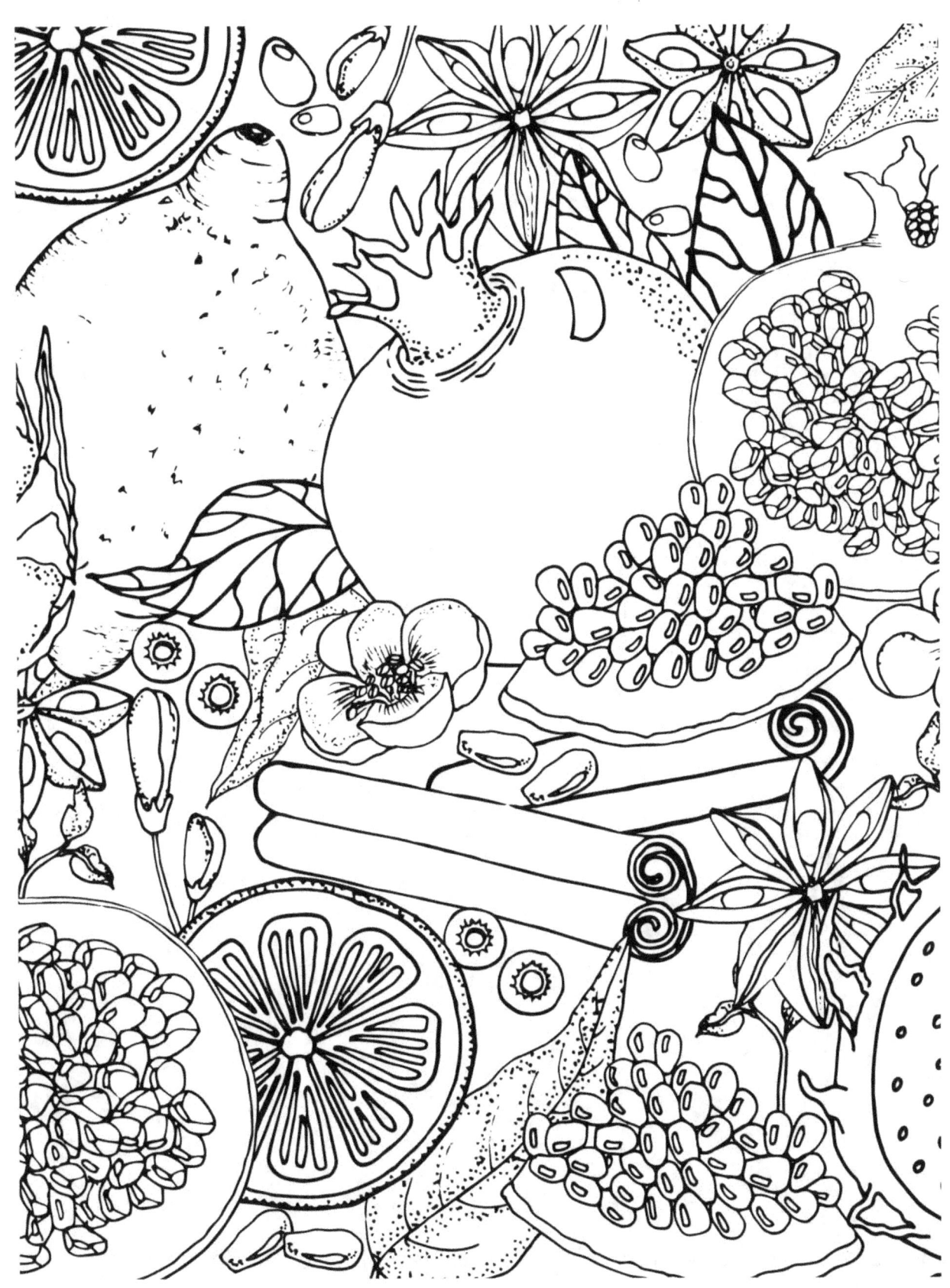

"He comes out like a flower and withers; he flees like a shadow and continues not."
(Job 14:2)

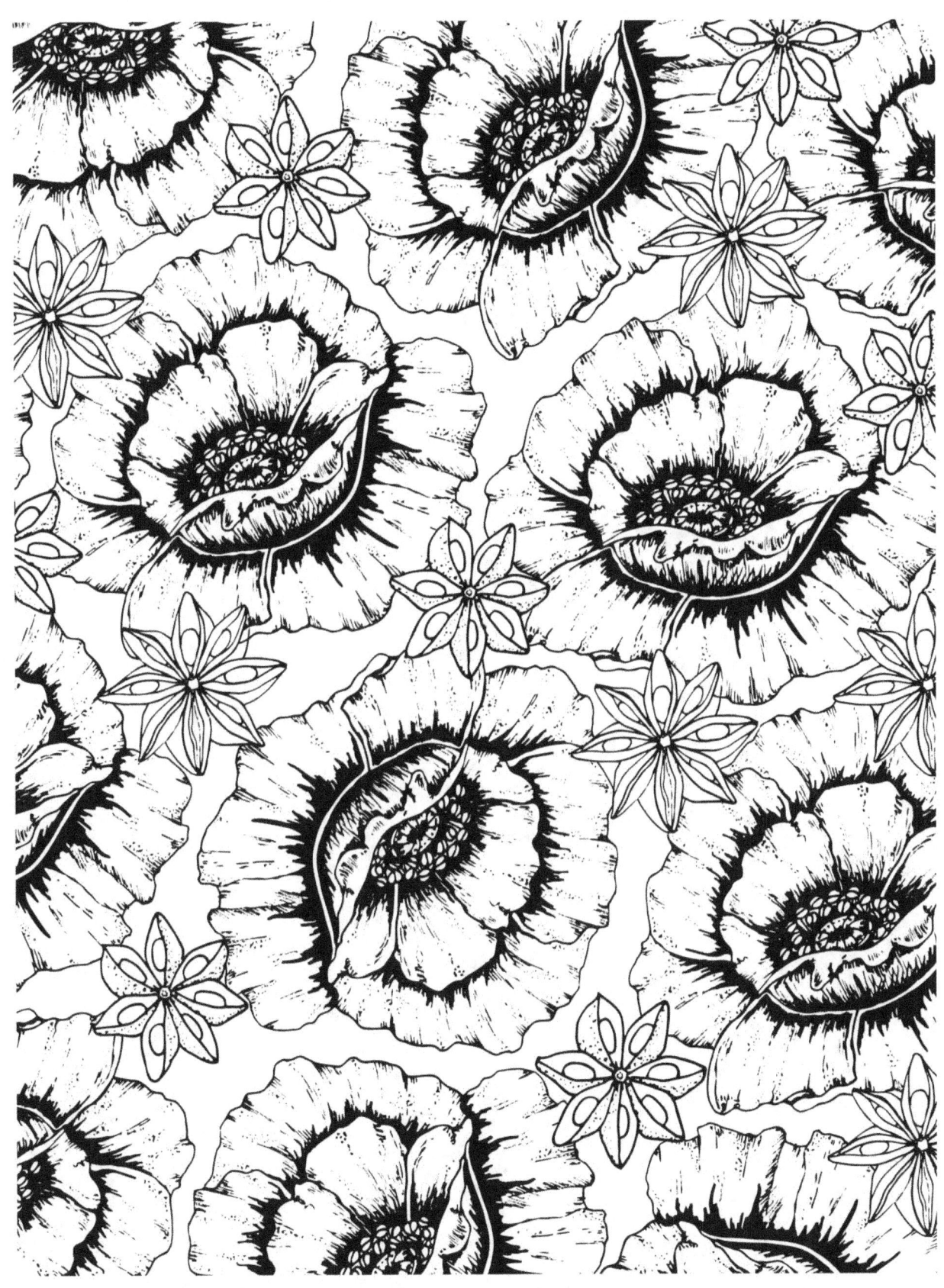

"His cheeks are like beds of spices, mounds of sweet-smelling herbs. His lips are lilies, dripping liquid myrrh." (Song of Solomon 5:13)

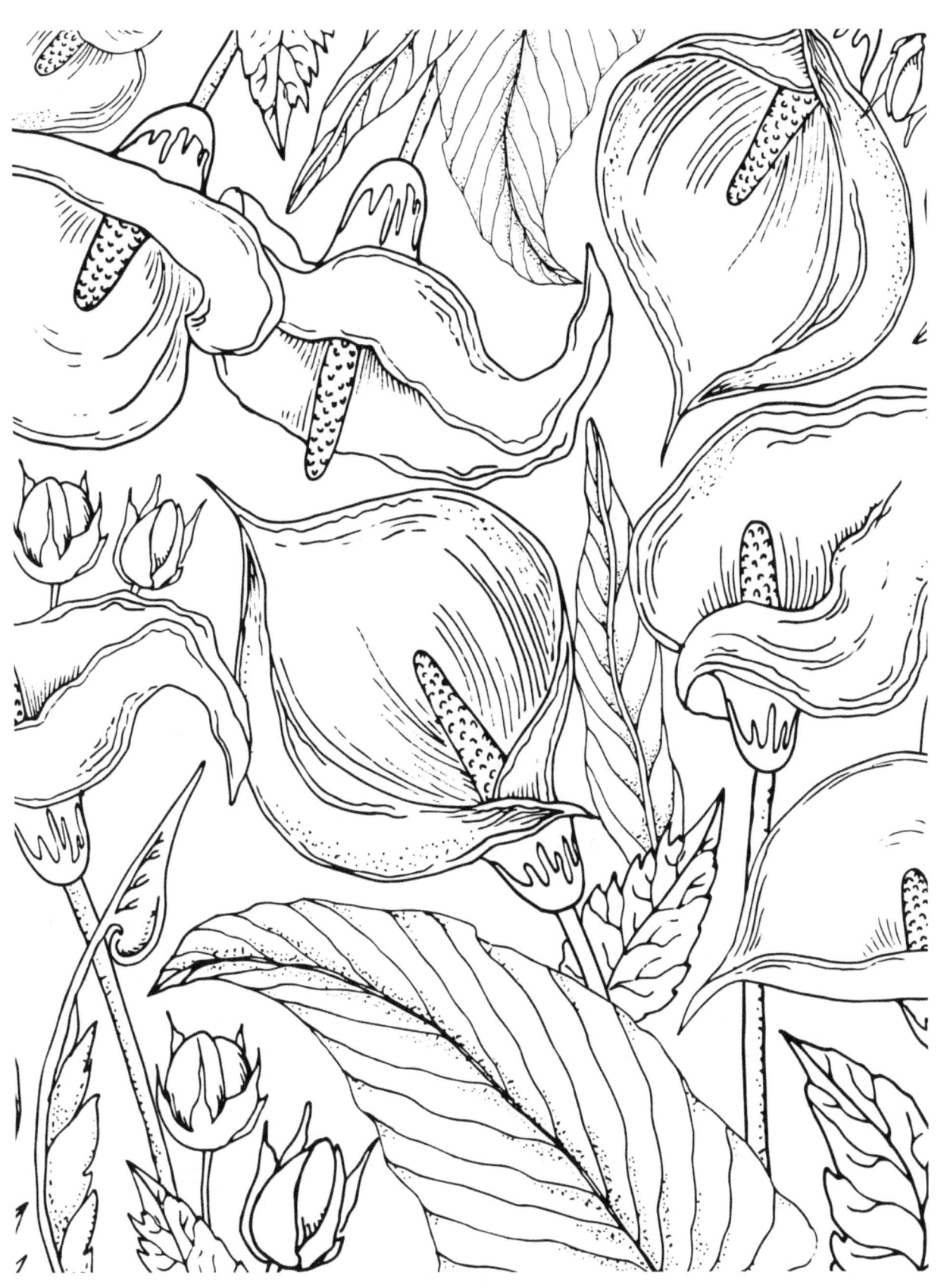

"Consider how the wild flowers grow." (Luke 12:27)

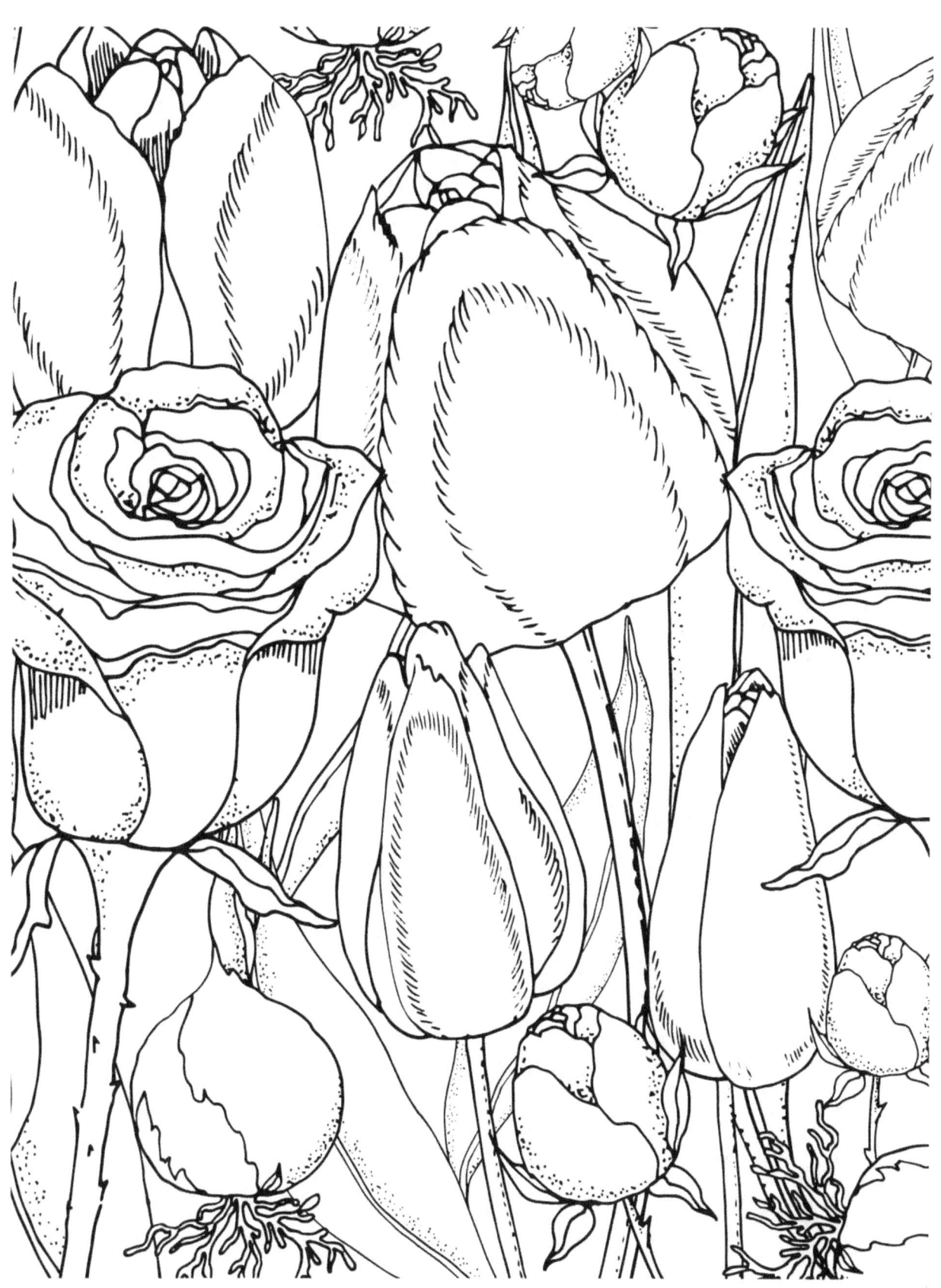

"I am the true vine." (John 15:1)

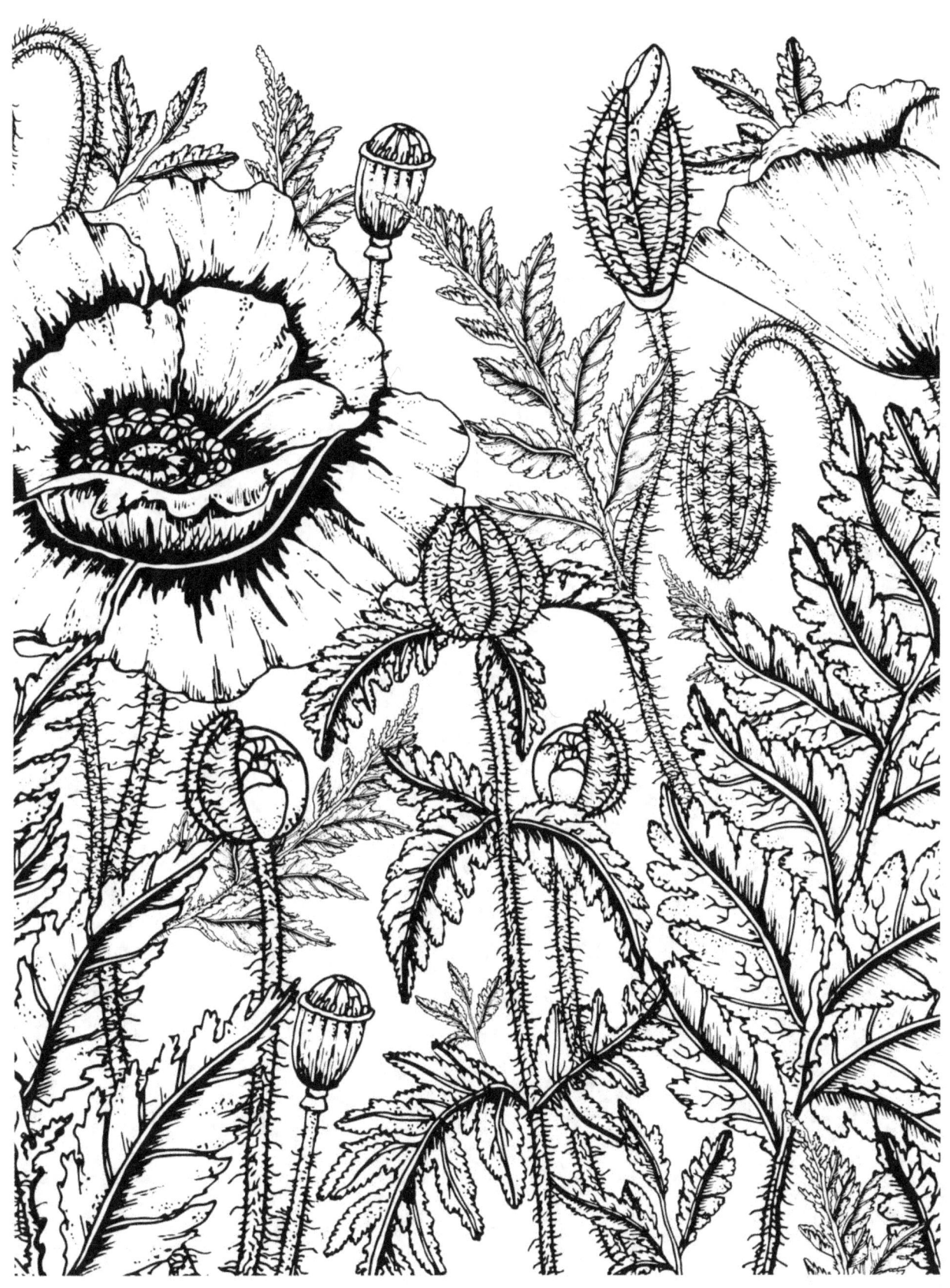

"Cultivate kindness." (Proverbs 3:3)

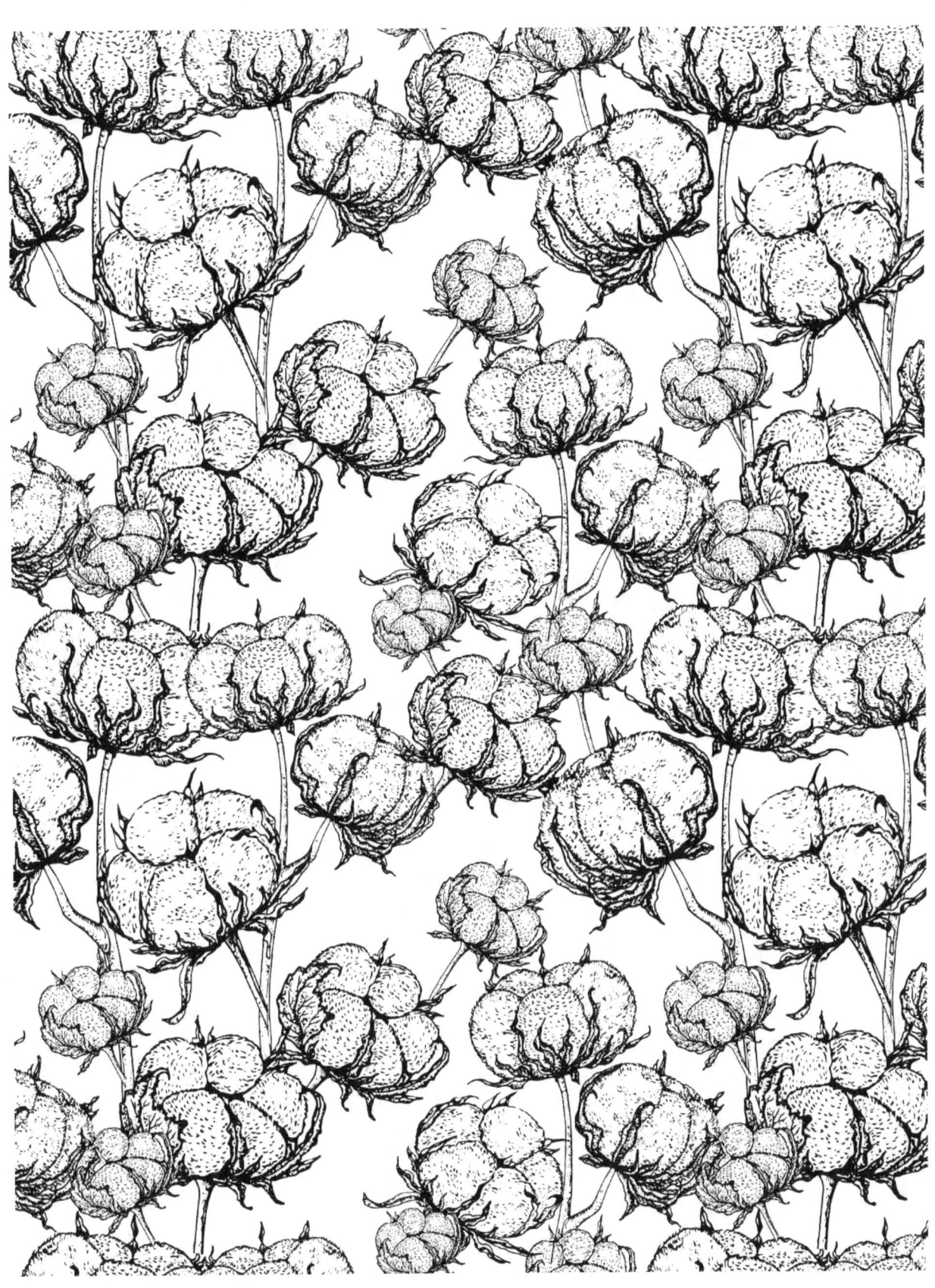

"...and you shall be like a watered garden, like a spring of water, whose waters fail not." (Isaiah 58:11b)

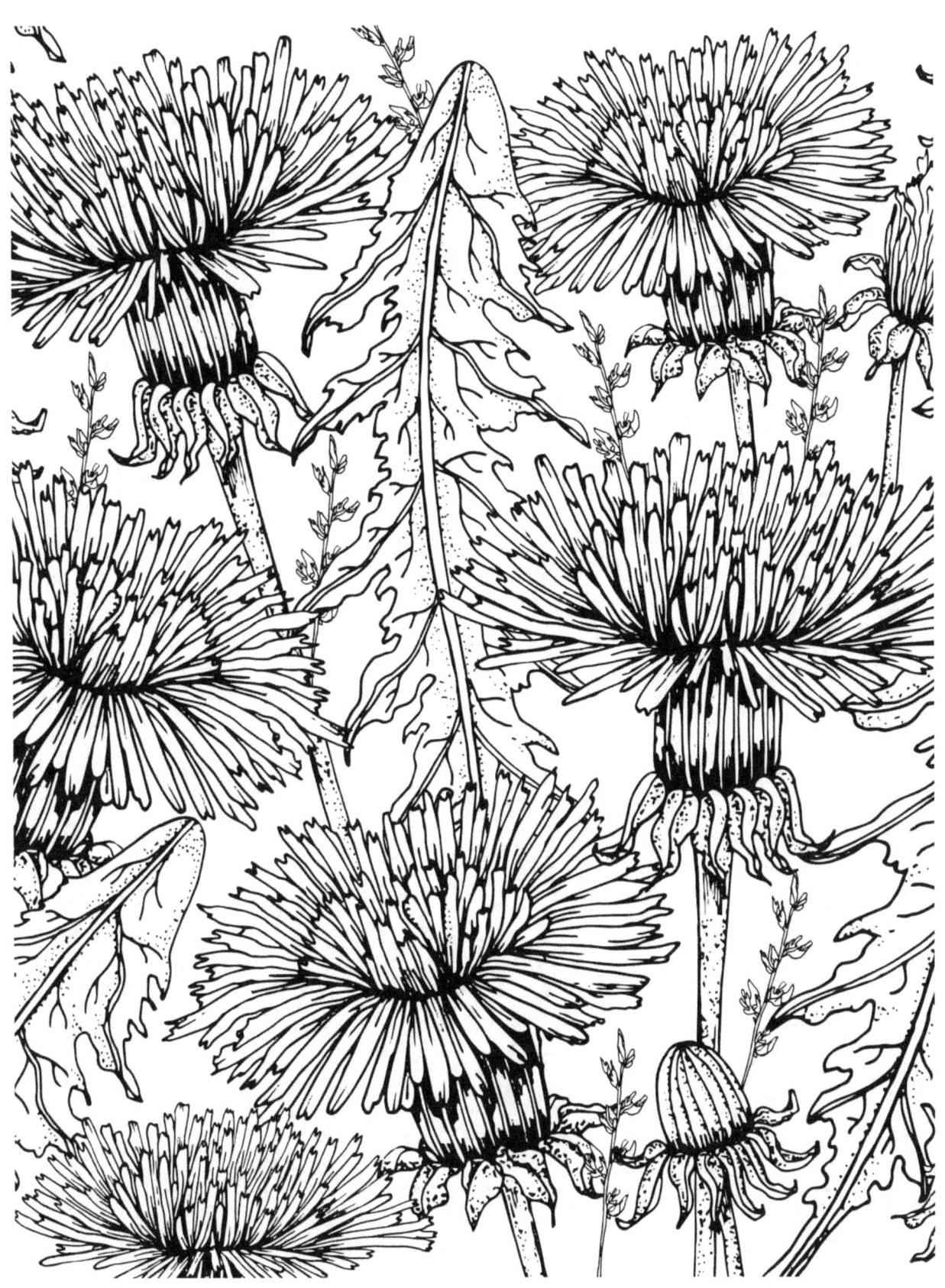

"Cast all your anxiety on Him, for He cares for you." (1 Peter 5:7)

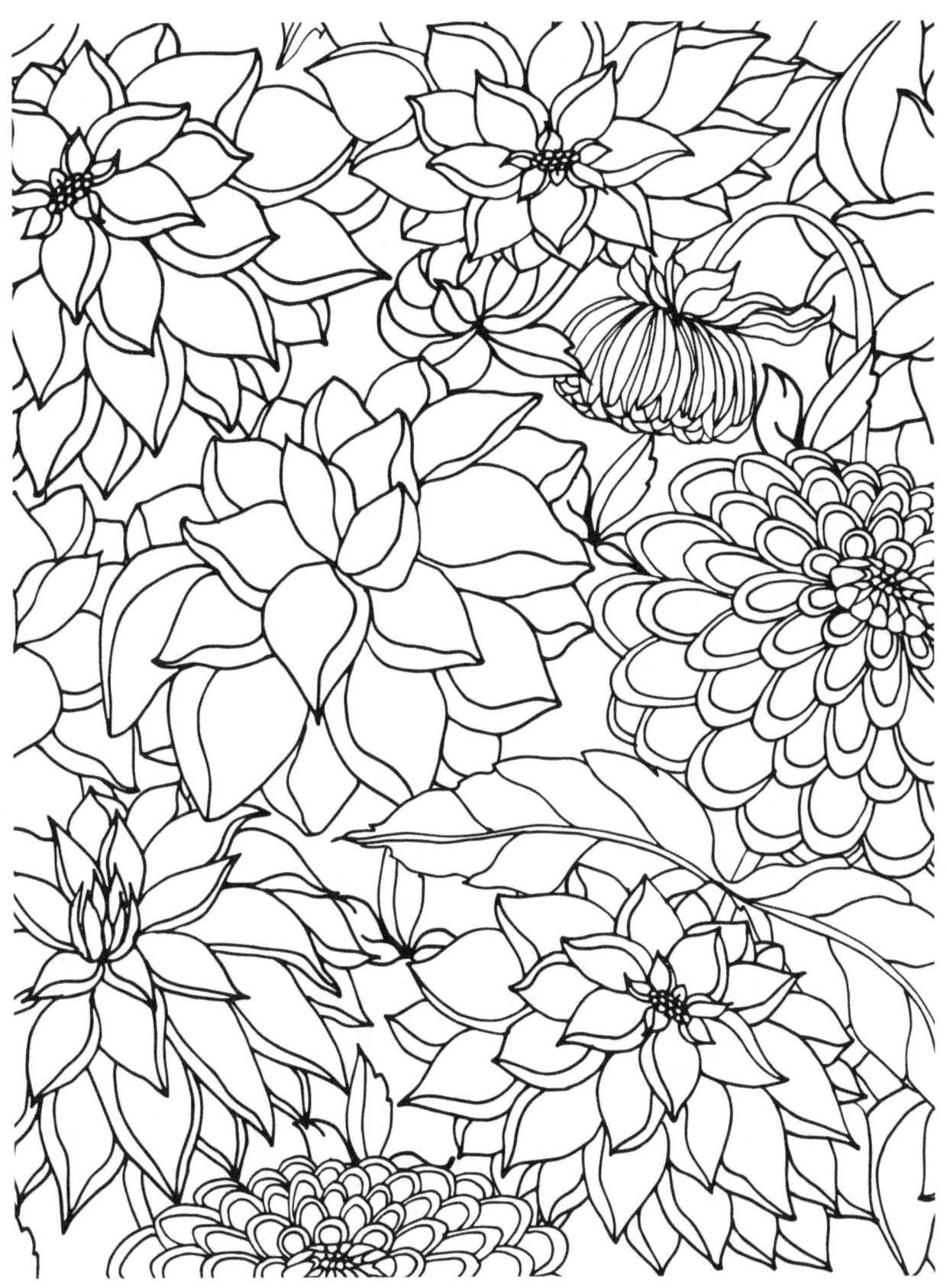

"A man reaps what he sows." (Galatians 6:7)

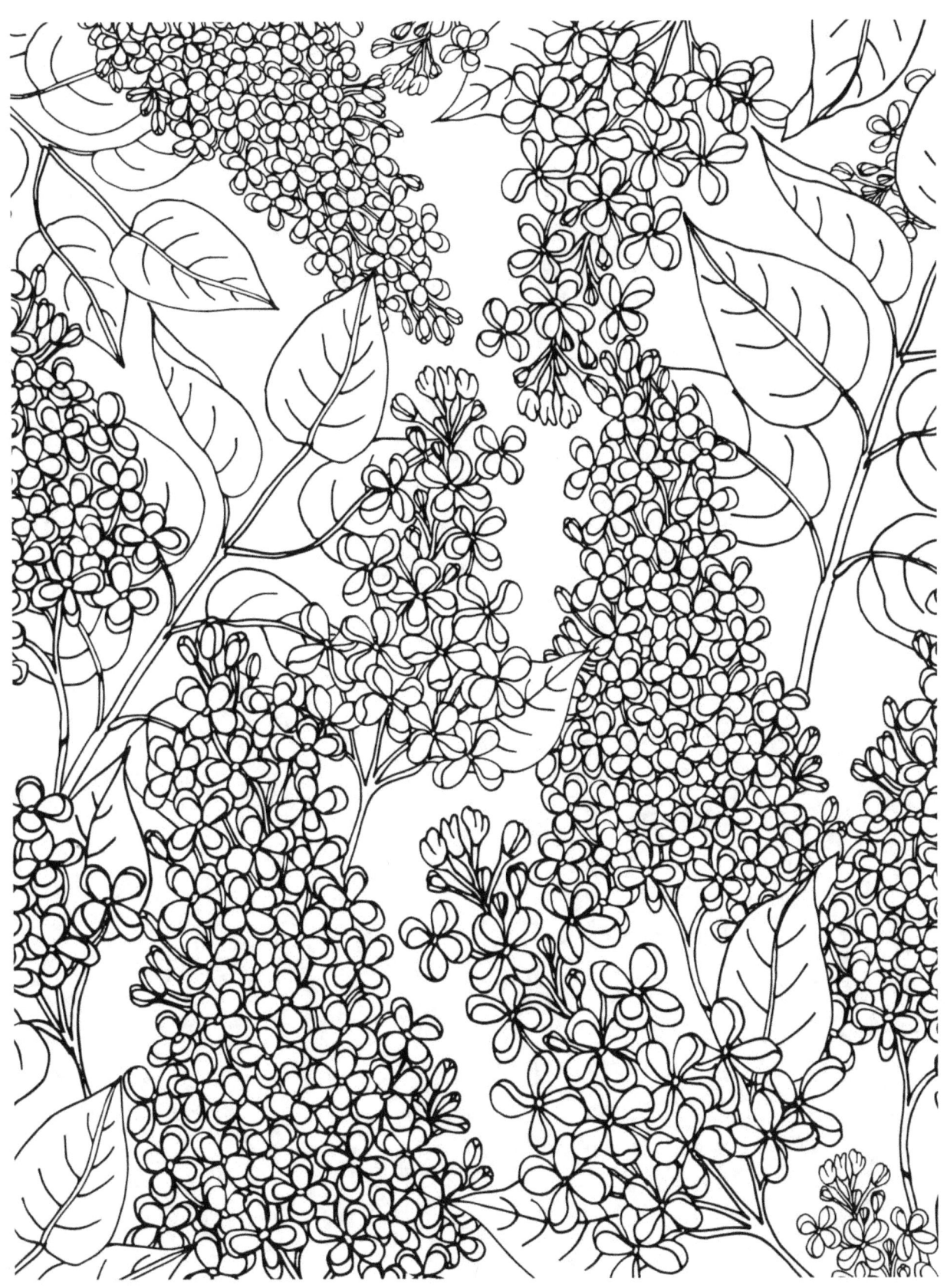

"Flowers are the music of the ground from earth's lips spoken without sound." (Edwin Curran)

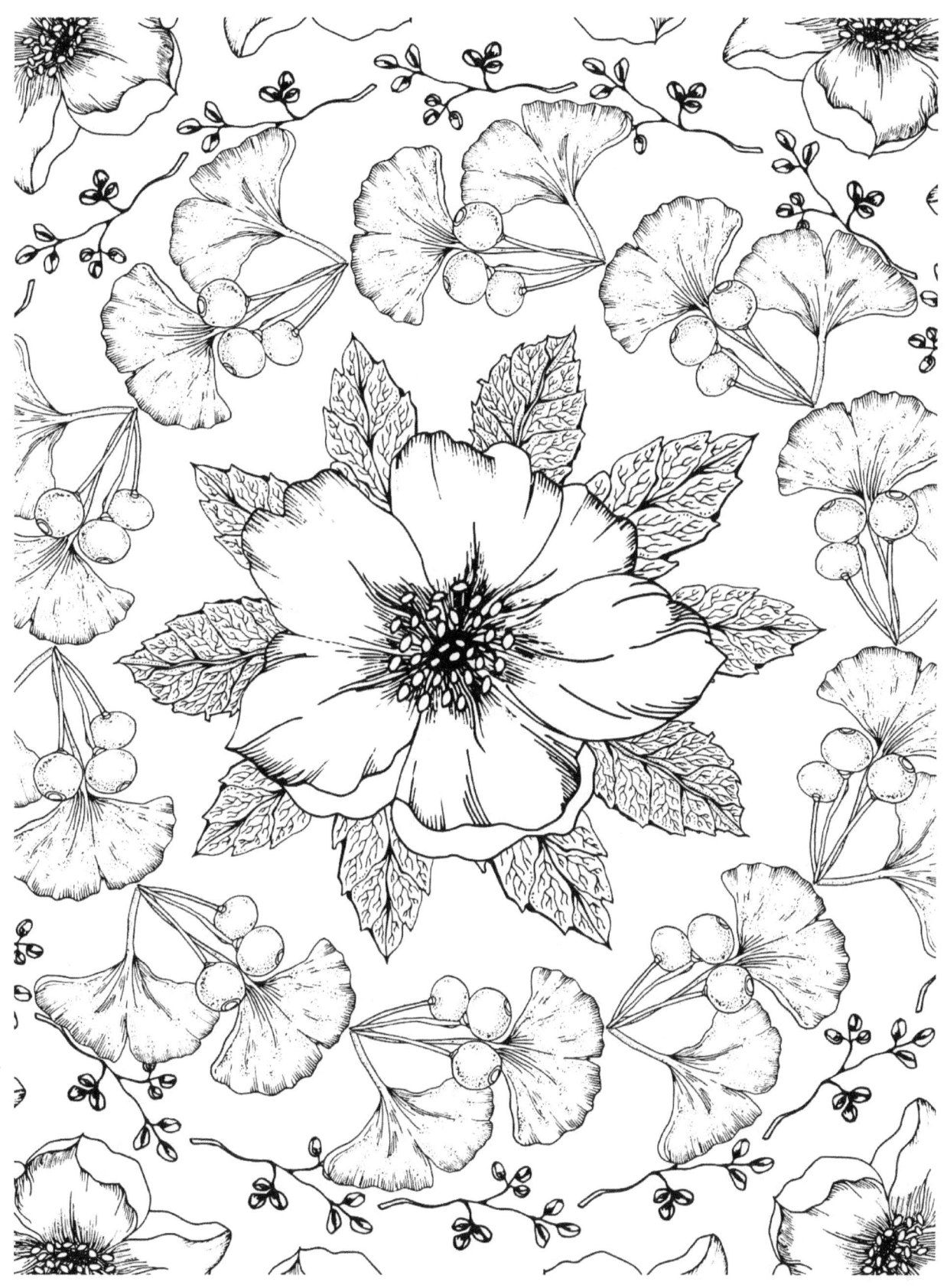

"God is in all creatures, even in the smallest flowers." (Martin Luther)

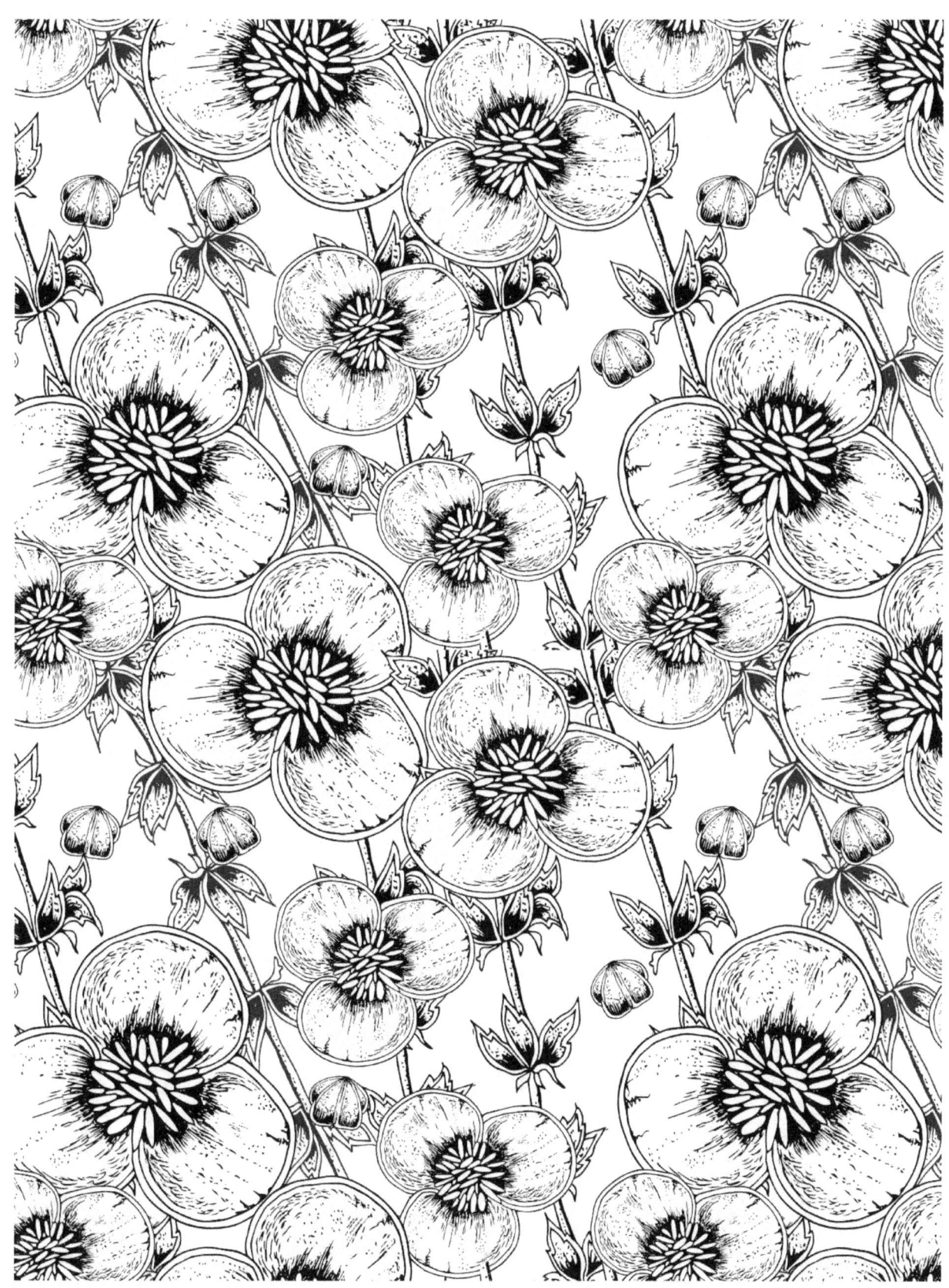

"For he knows how we are formed, he remembers that we are dust. The life of mortals is like grass, they flourish like a flower of the field; the wind blows over it and it is gone, and its place remembers it no more." (Psalm 103:14-15)

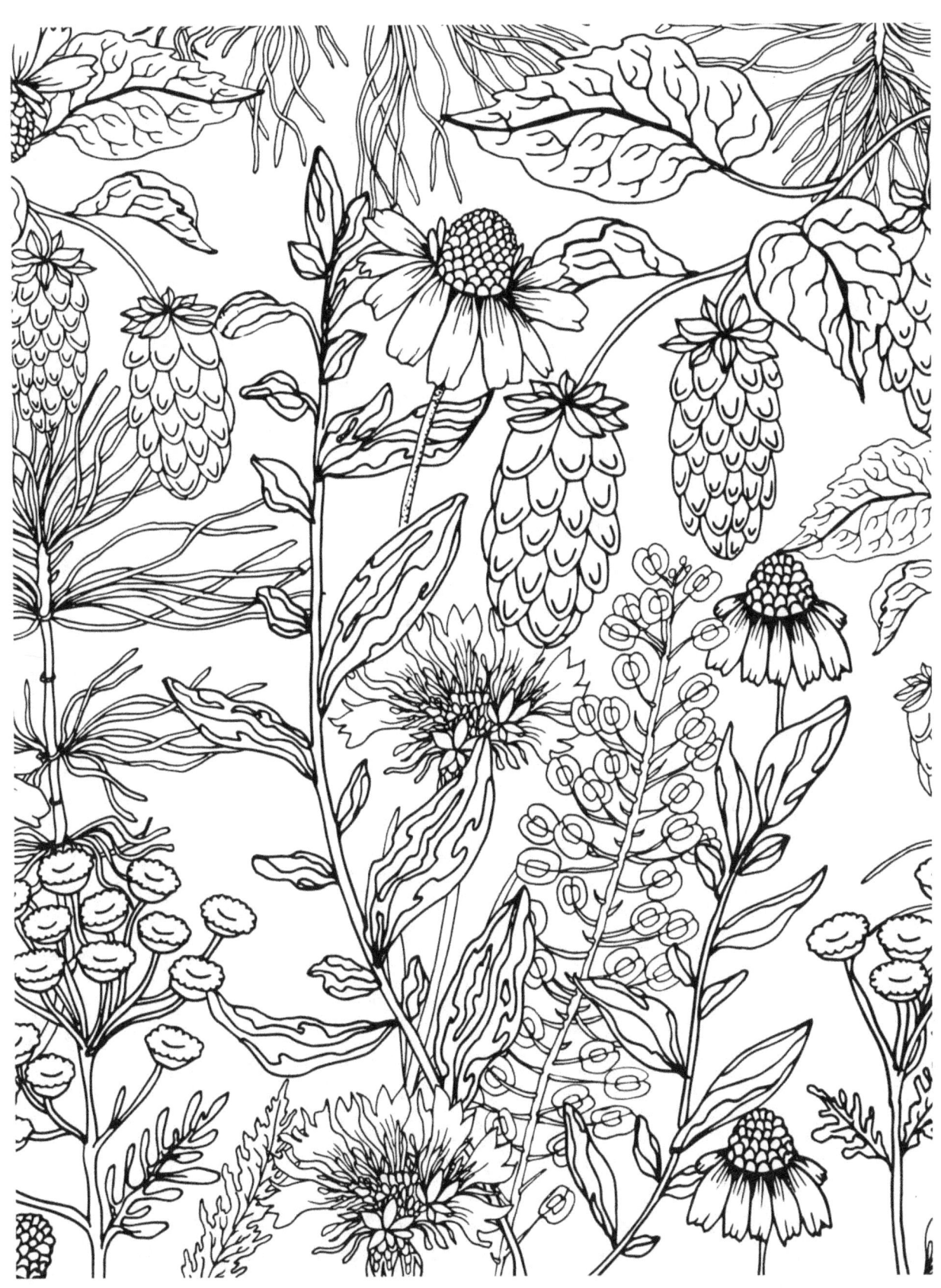

"It sits at the head of a fertile valley, but its glorious beauty will fade like a flower. Whoever sees it will snatch it up, as an early fig is quickly picked and eaten." (Isaiah 28:4)

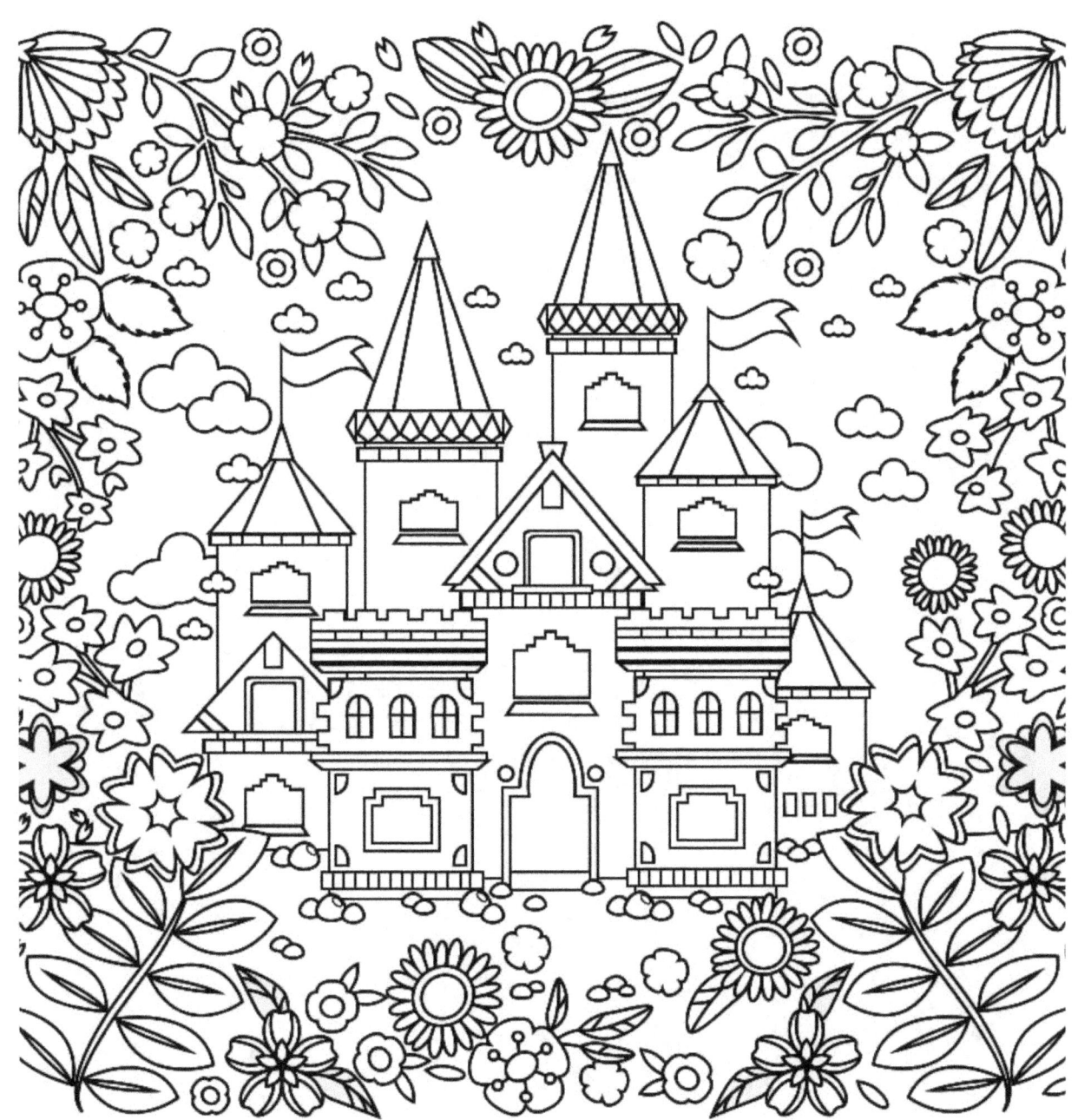

"For, All people are like grass, and all their glory is like the flowers of the field; the grass withers and the flowers fall." (1 Peter 1:24)

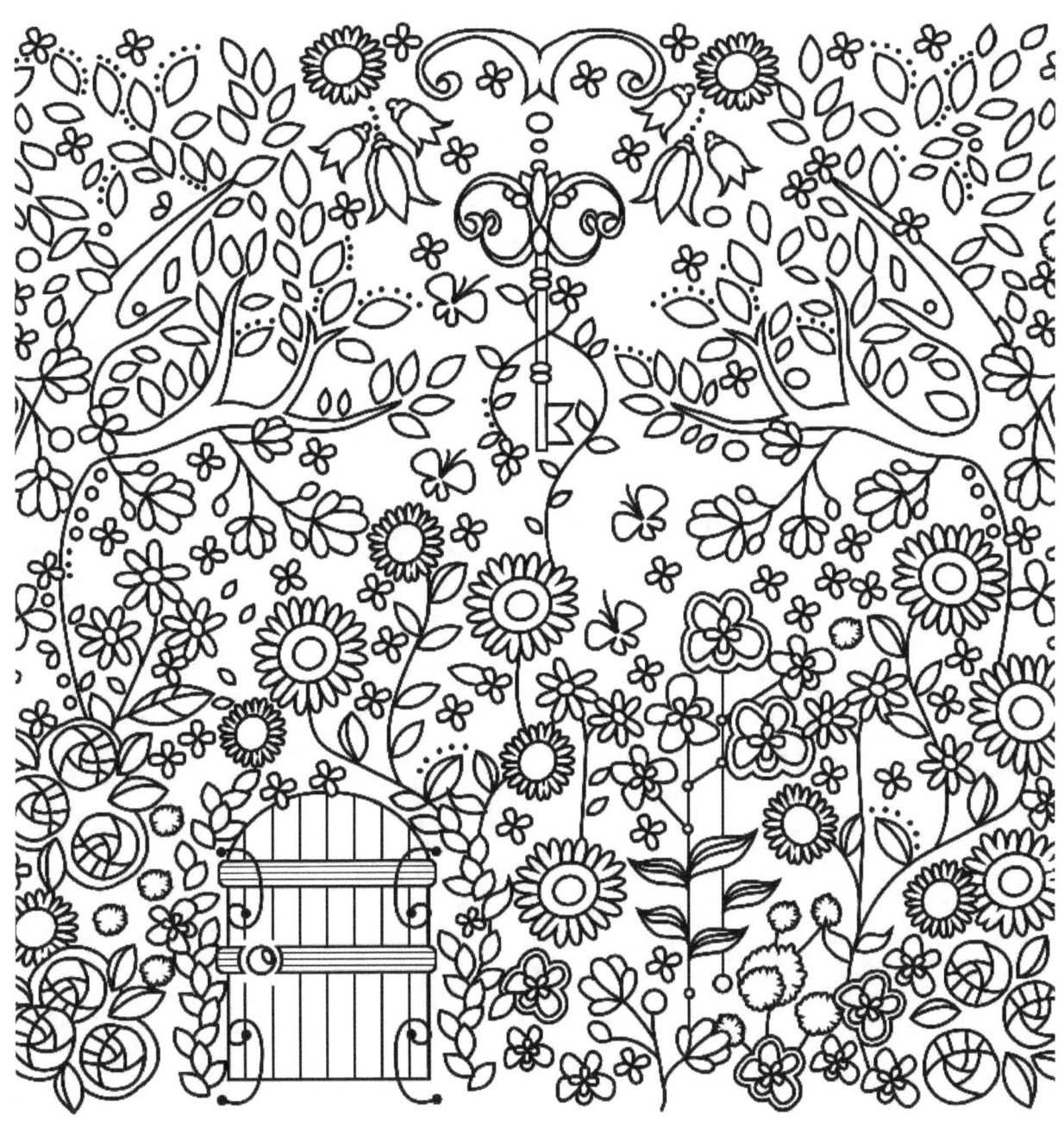

"A voice says, "Cry out." And I said, "What shall I cry?" "All people are like grass, and all their faithfulness is like the flowers of the field." (Isaiah 40:6)

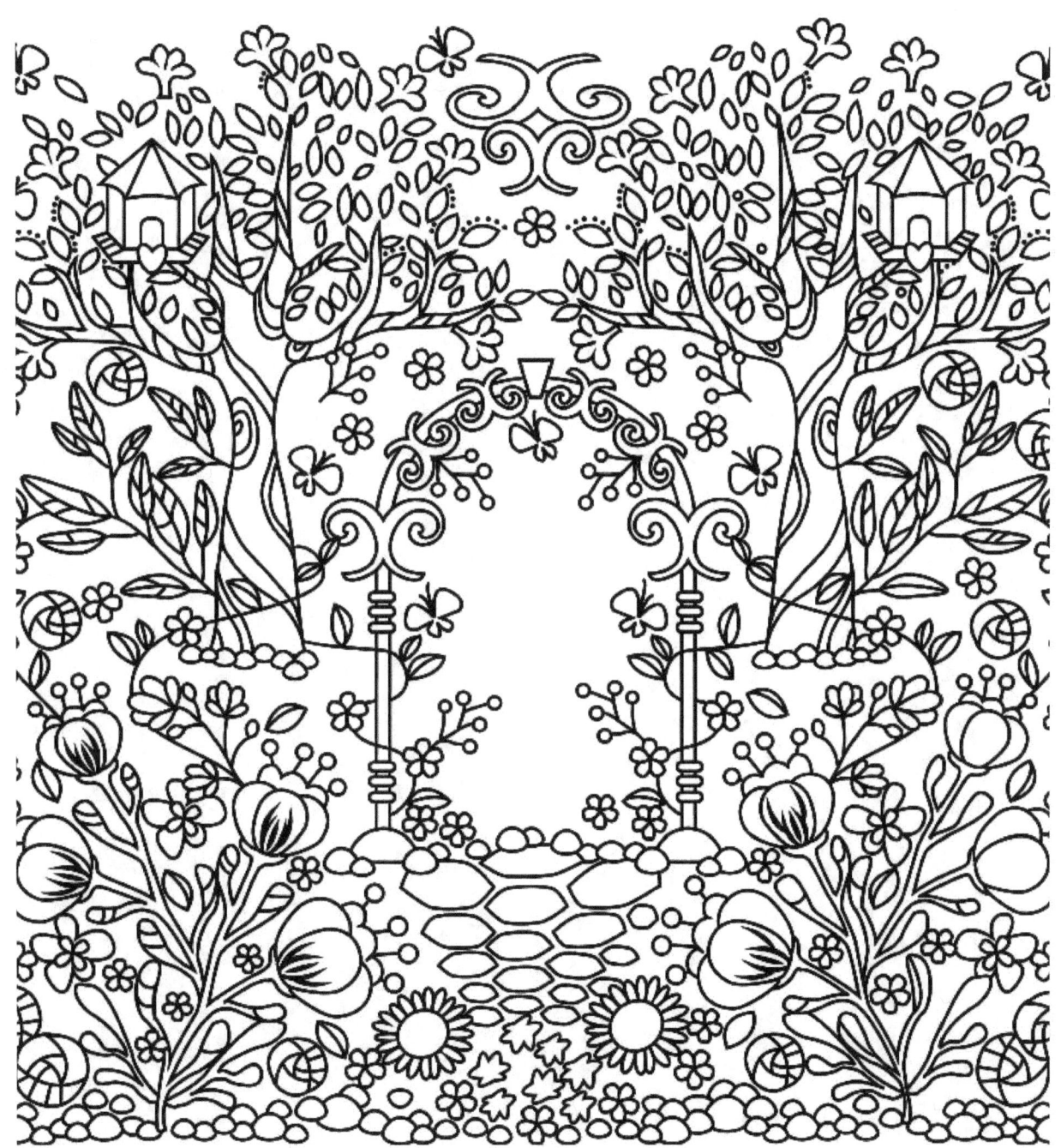

"The grass withers and the flowers fall, but the word of our God endures forever."
(Isaiah 40:8)

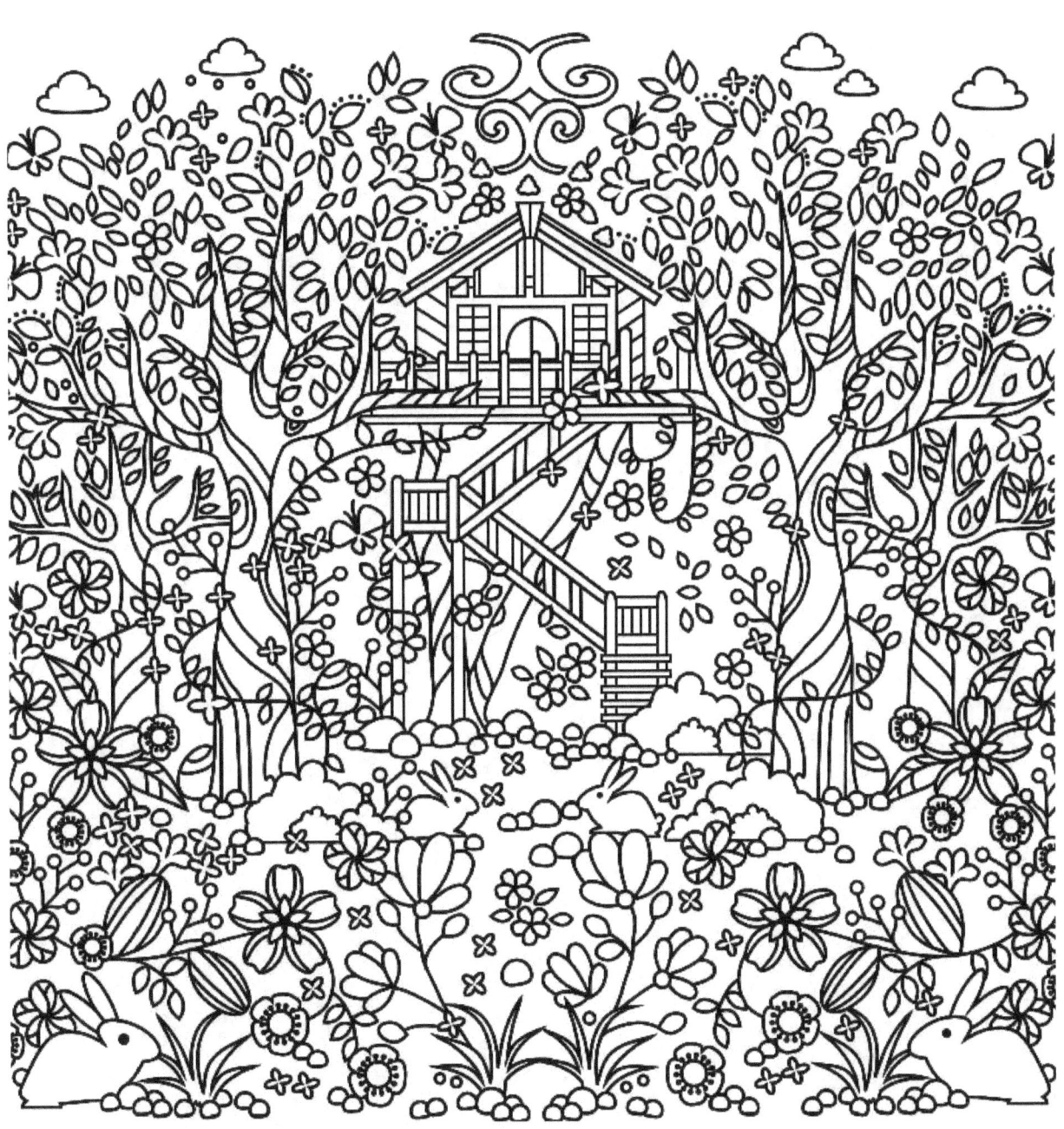

"Mortals, born of woman, are of few days and full of trouble. They spring up like flowers and wither away; like fleeting shadows, they do not endure." (Job 14:1-2)

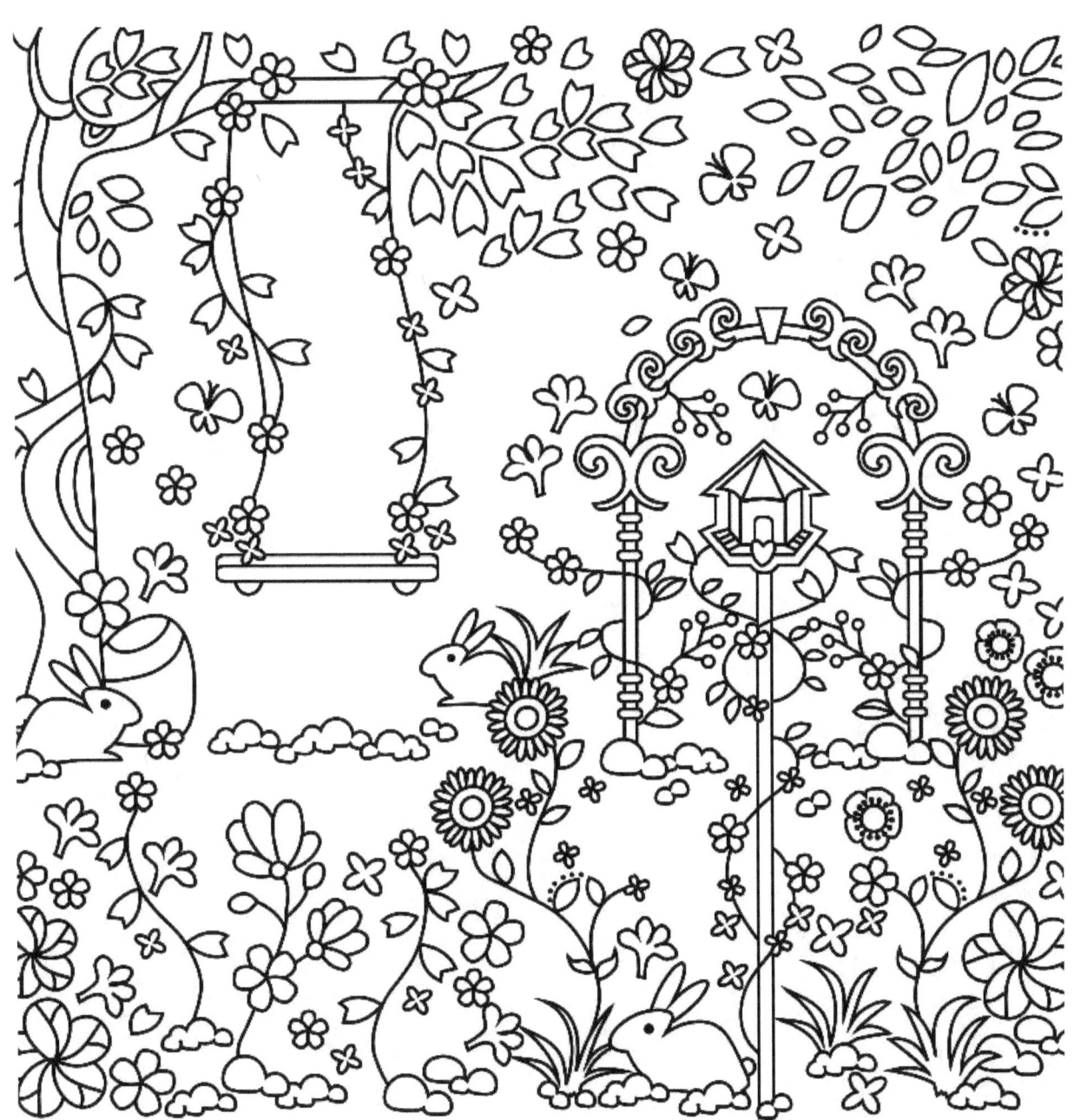

"Look at the lilies and how they grow. They don't work or make their clothing, yet Solomon in all his glory was not dressed as beautifully as they are. And if God cares so wonderfully for flowers that are here today and thrown into the fire tomorrow, he will certainly care for you. Why do you have so little faith?" (Luke 12:27-28)

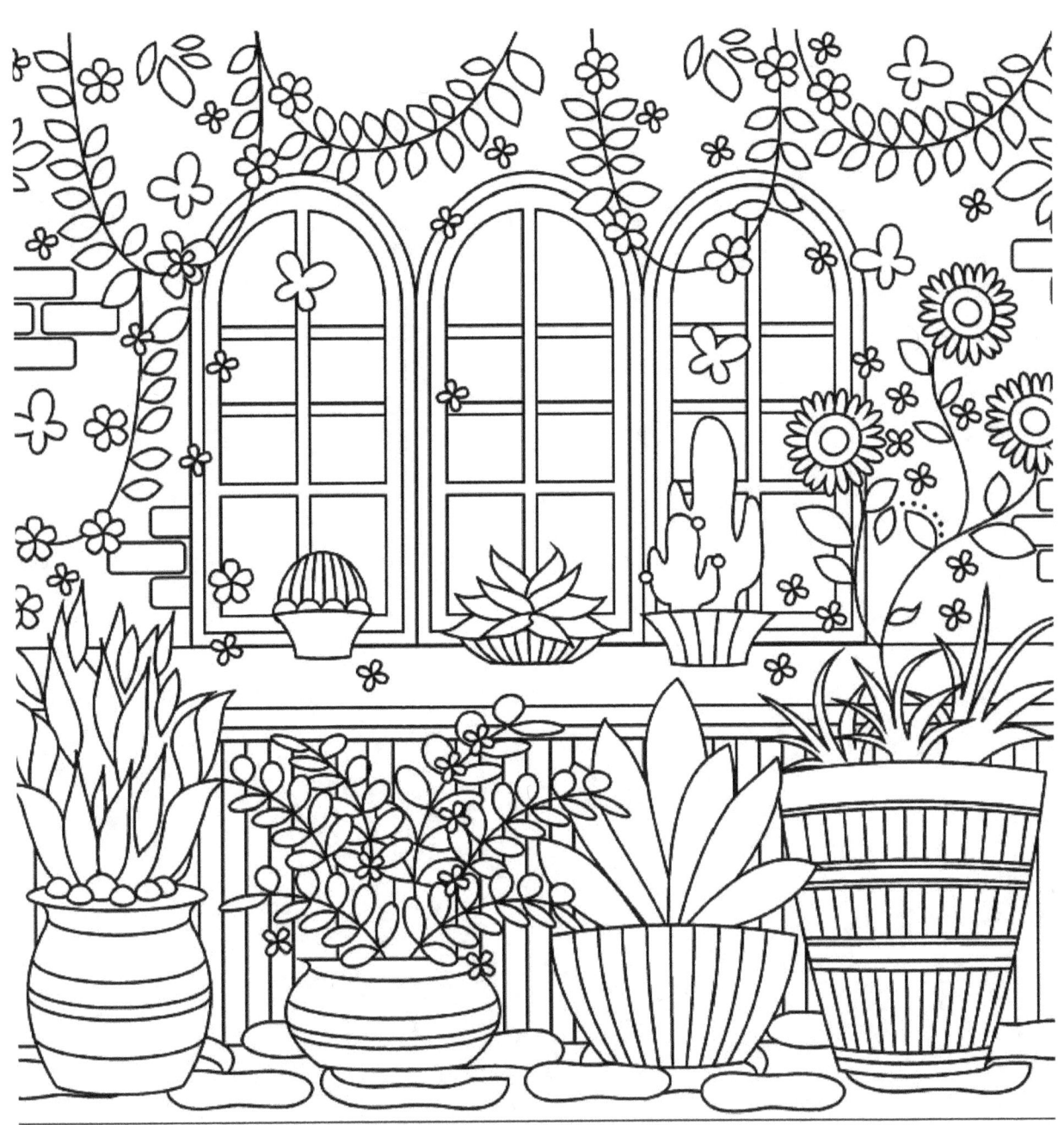

"But grow in the grace and knowledge of our Lord and Savior Jesus Christ. To him be the honor both now and on that eternal day."(2 Peter 3:18)

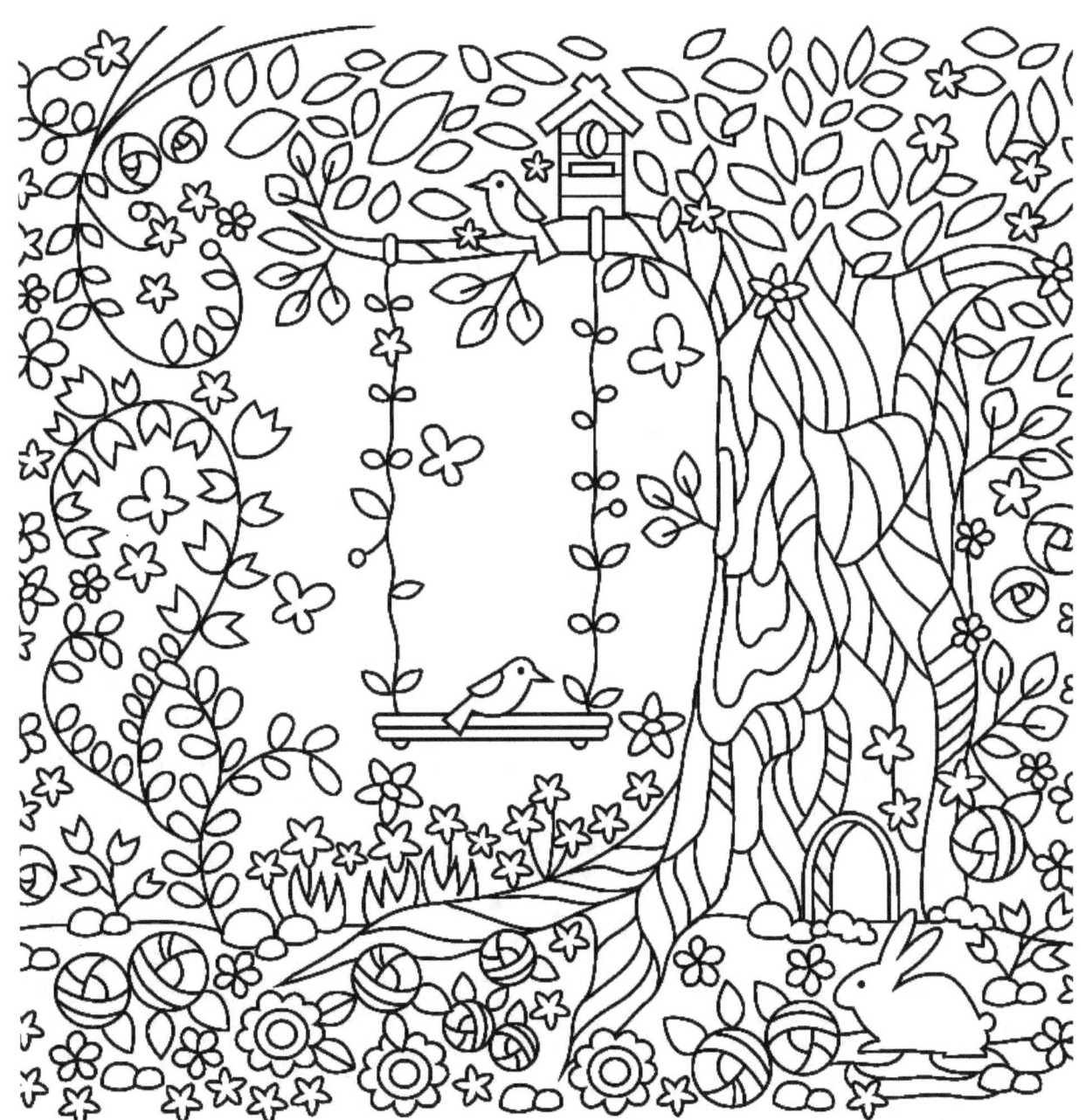

"The fig tree has ripened its figs, and the vines in blossom have given forth their fragrance. Arise, my darling, my beautiful one, and come along!" (Song of Solomon 2:3)

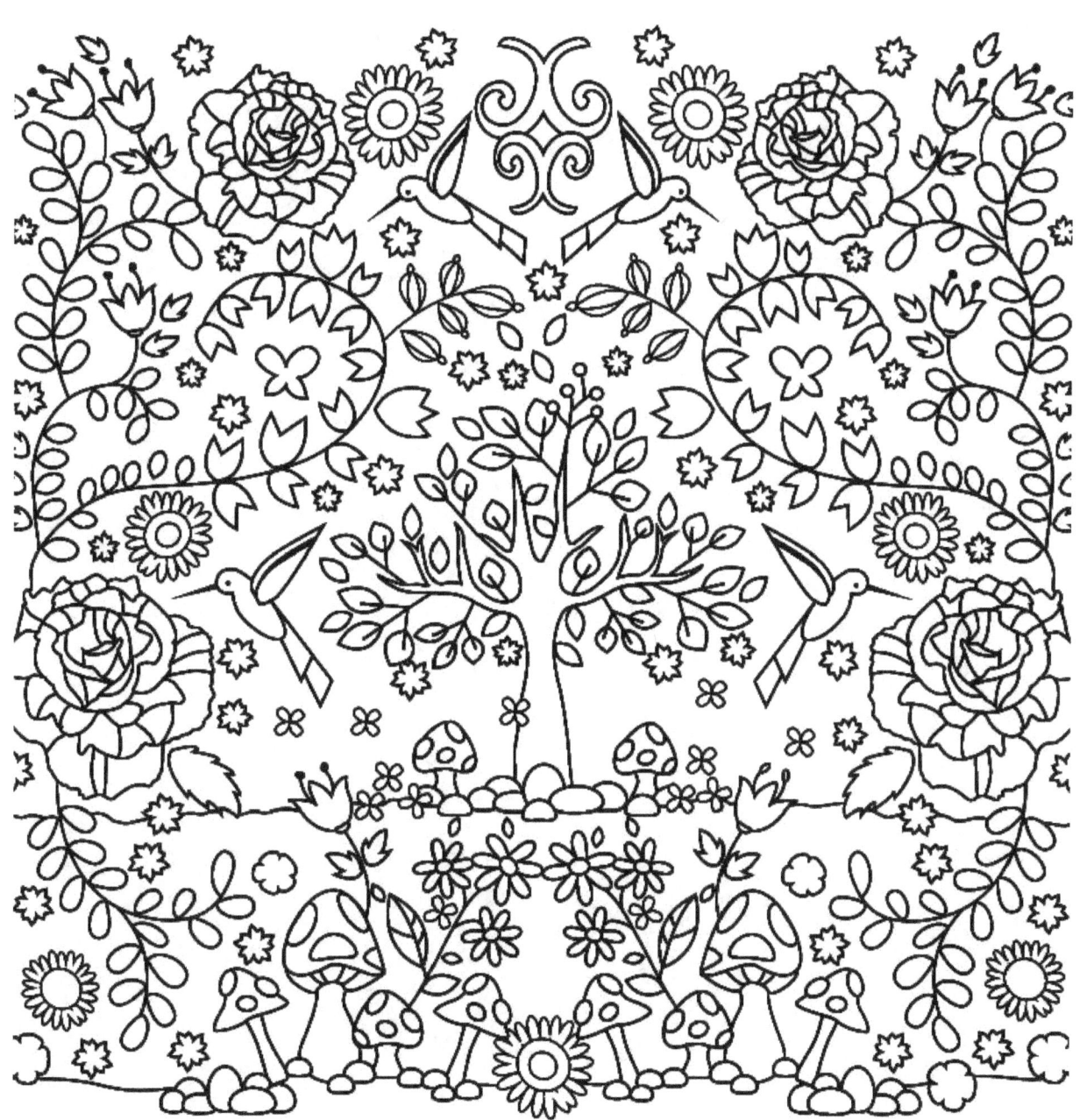

"Under the lotus plants he lies, in the shelter of the reeds and in the marsh." (Job 40:21)

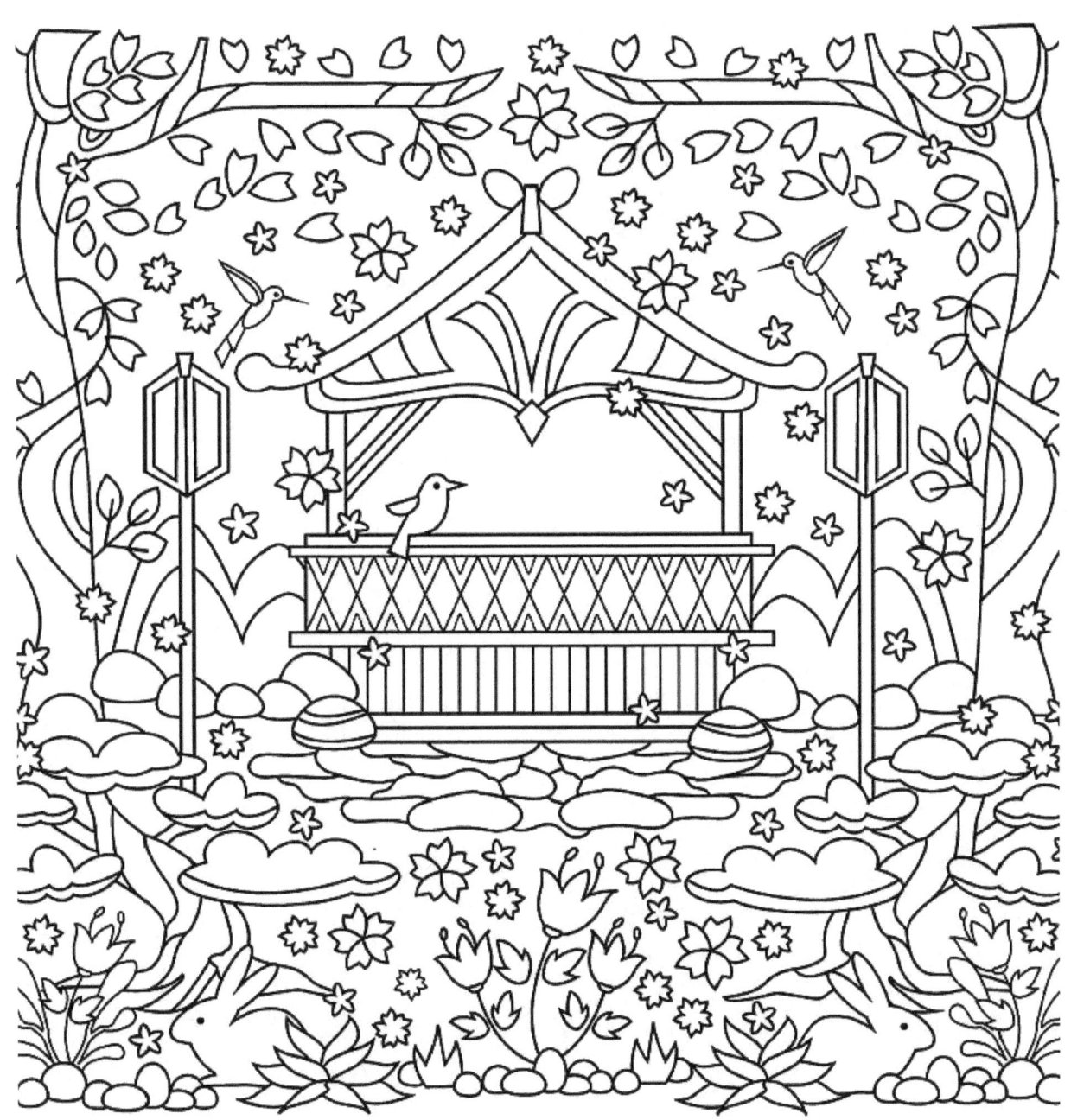

"He makes me lie down in green pastures. He leads me beside still waters. He restores my soul. He leads me in paths of righteousness for his name's sake." (Psalm 23:2-3)

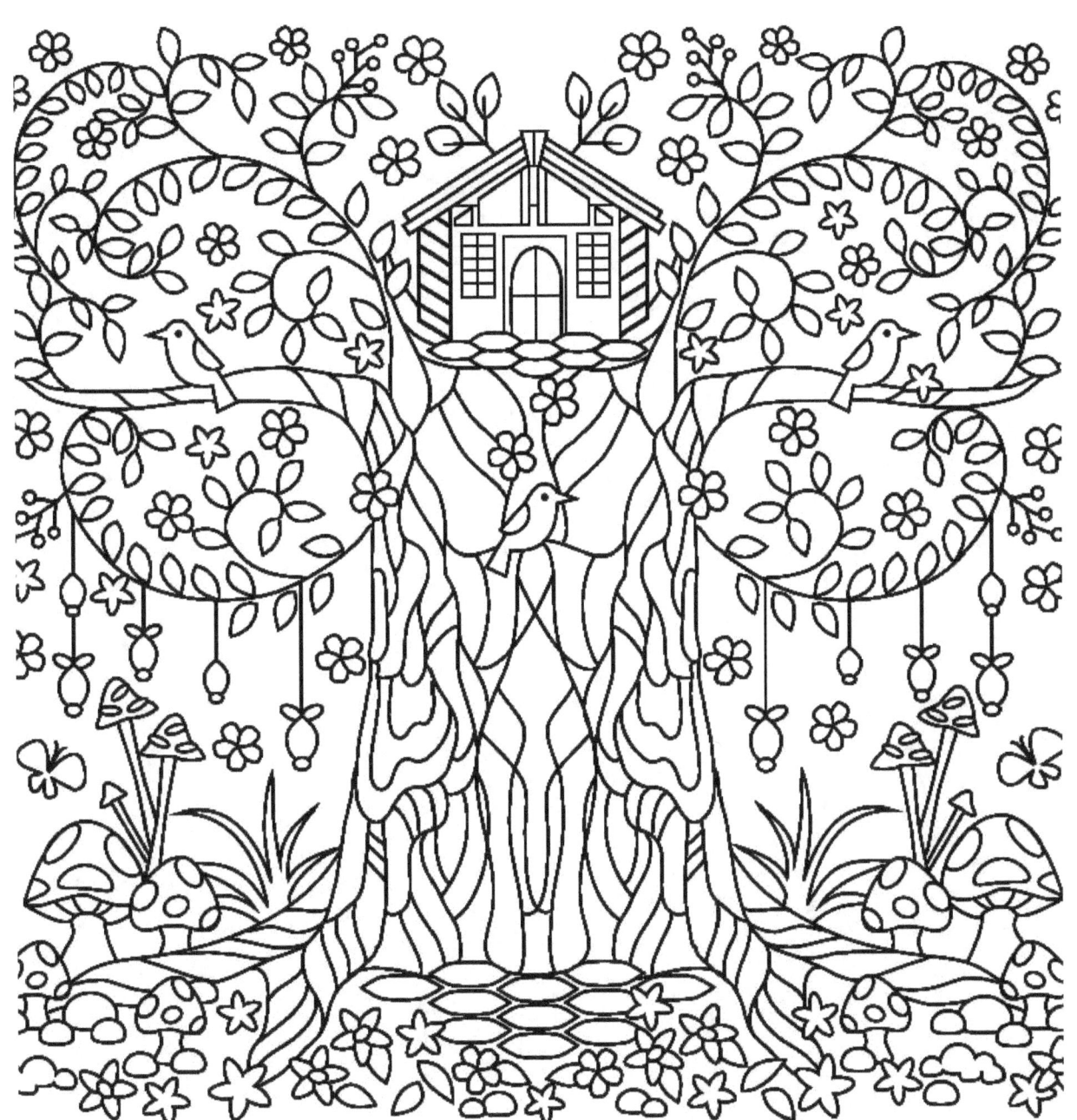

"On them he carved cherubim and palm trees and open flowers, and he overlaid them with gold evenly applied on the carved work." (1 Kings 6:35)

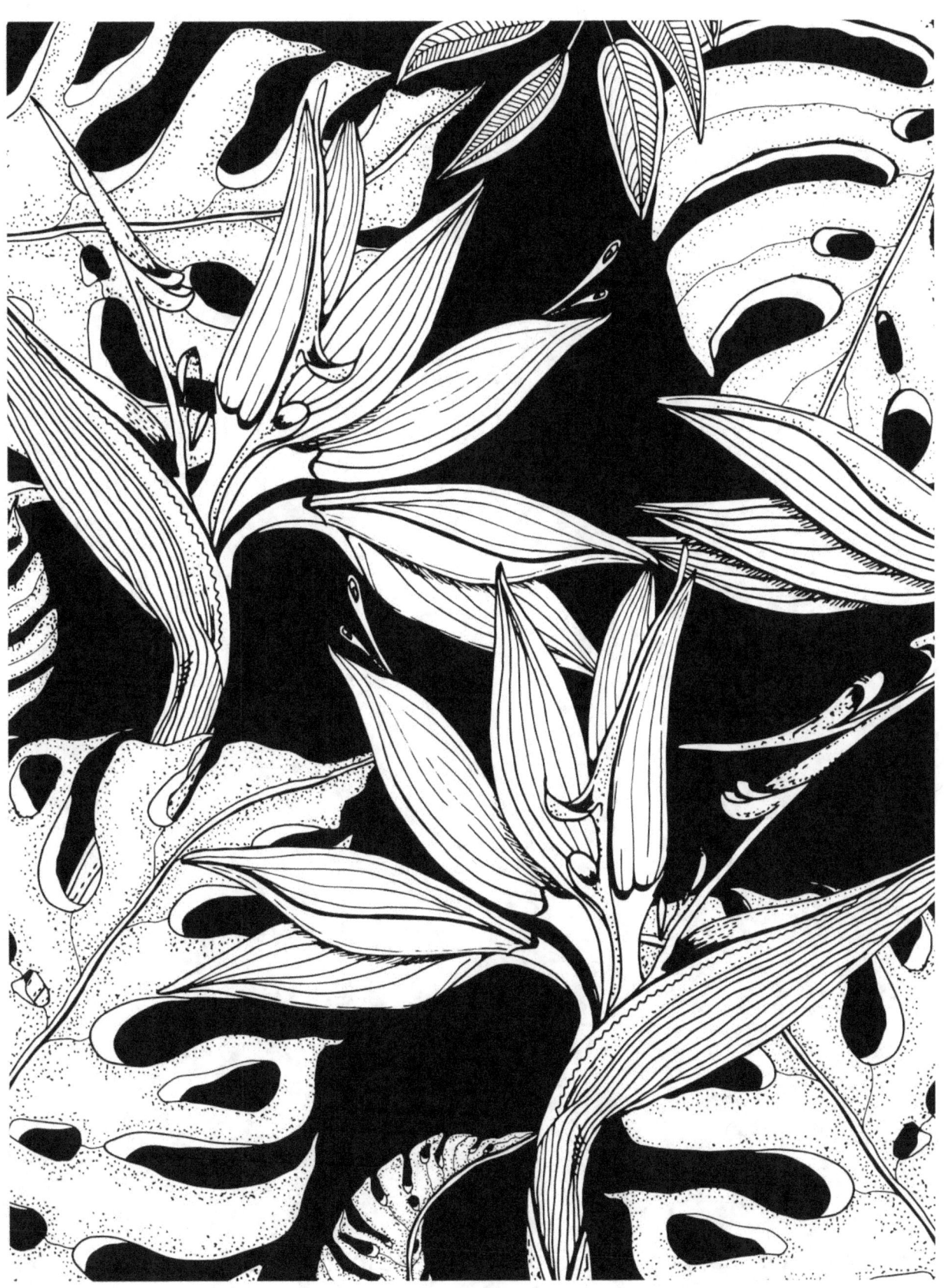

"Purge me with hyssop, and I shall be clean; wash me, and I shall be whiter than snow." (Psalm 51:7)

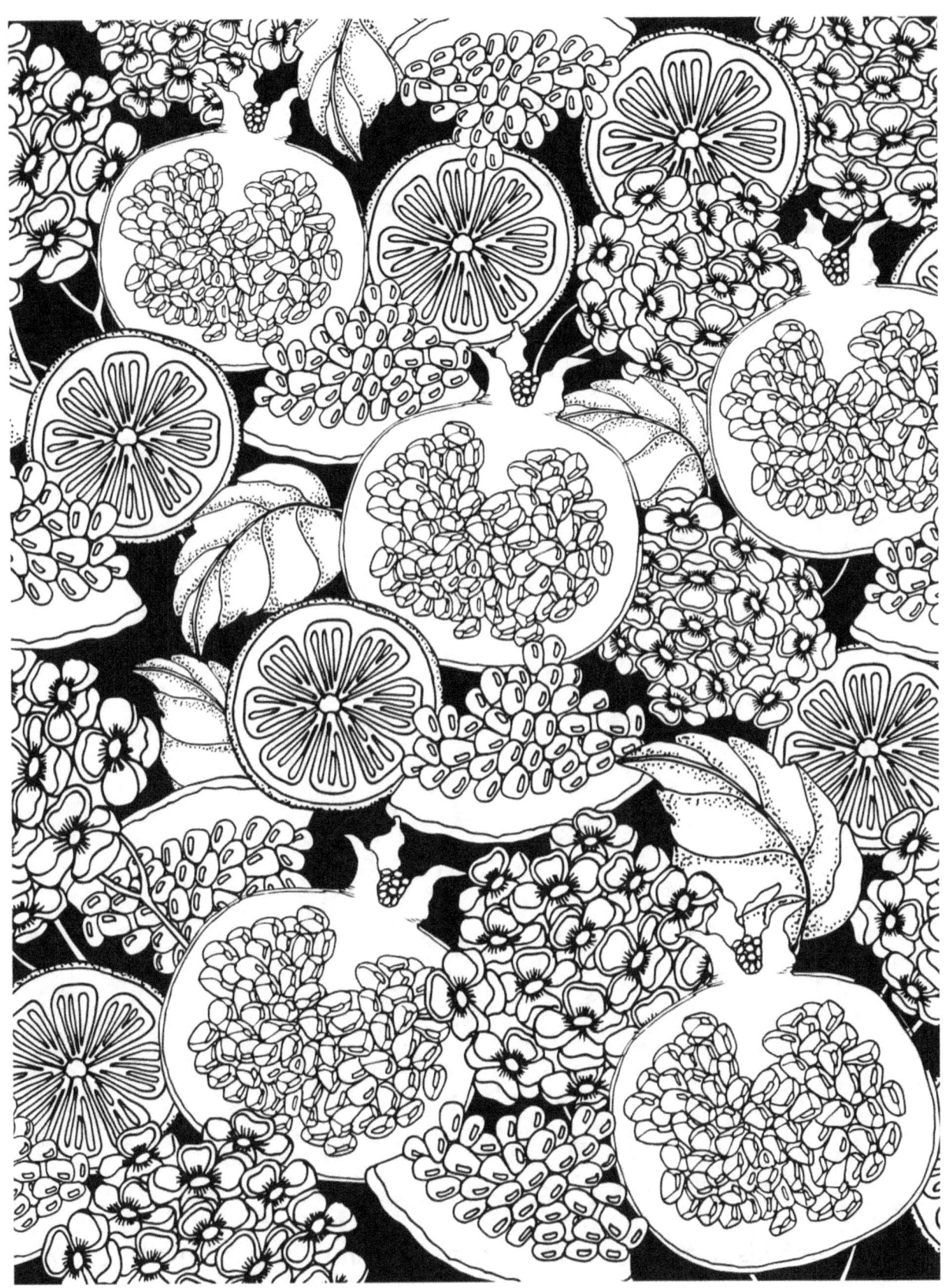

"He will shake off his unripe grape like the vine, and cast off his blossom like the olive tree." (Job 15:33)

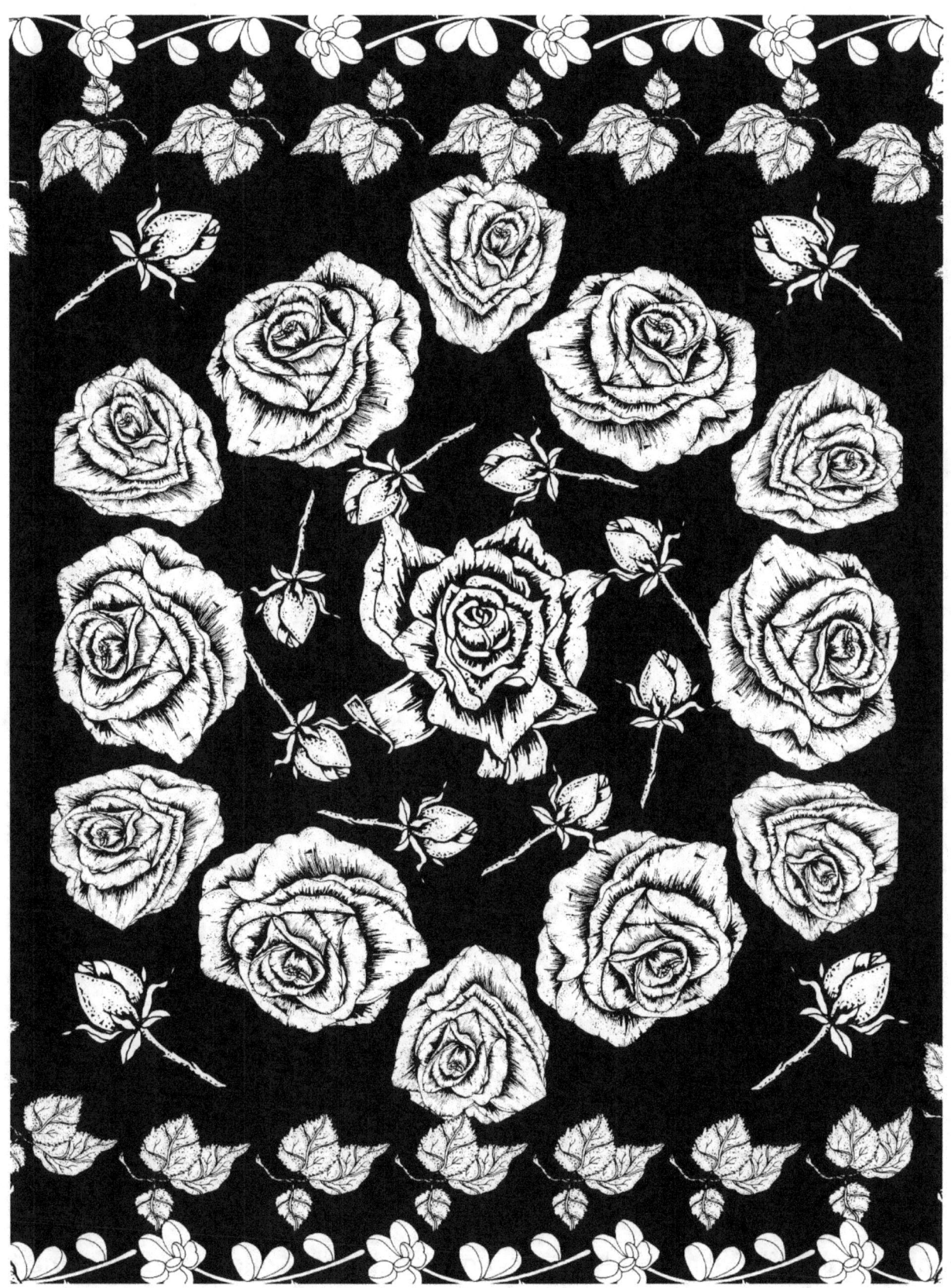

"Three cups made like almond blossoms, each with calyx and flower, on one branch, and three cups made like almond blossoms, each with calyx and flower, on the other branch—so for the six branches going out of the lampstand." (Exodus 37:19)

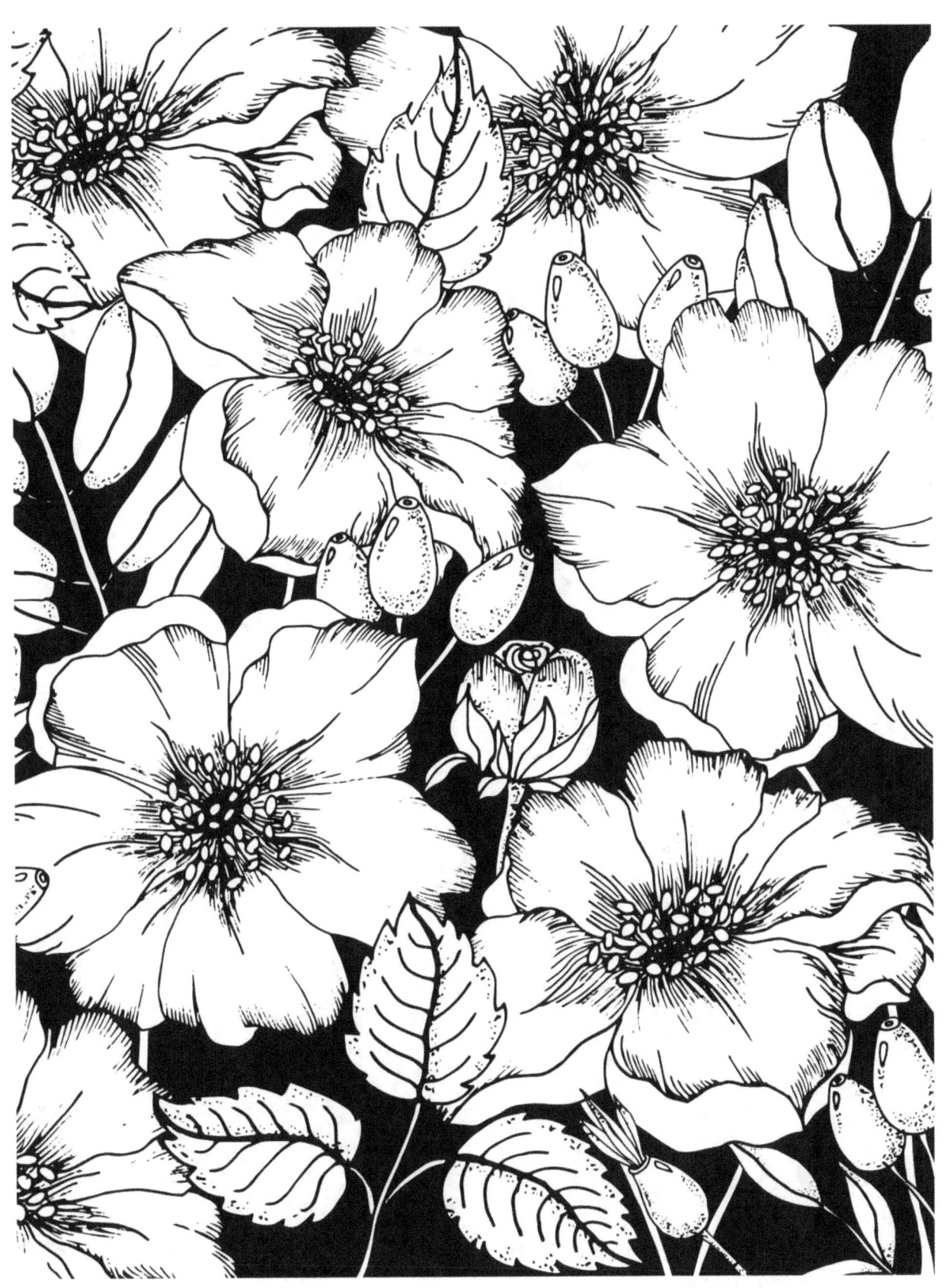

"Instead of the thorn shall come up the cypress; instead of the brier shall come up the myrtle; and it shall make a name for the Lord, an everlasting sign that shall not be cut off." (Isaiah 55:13)

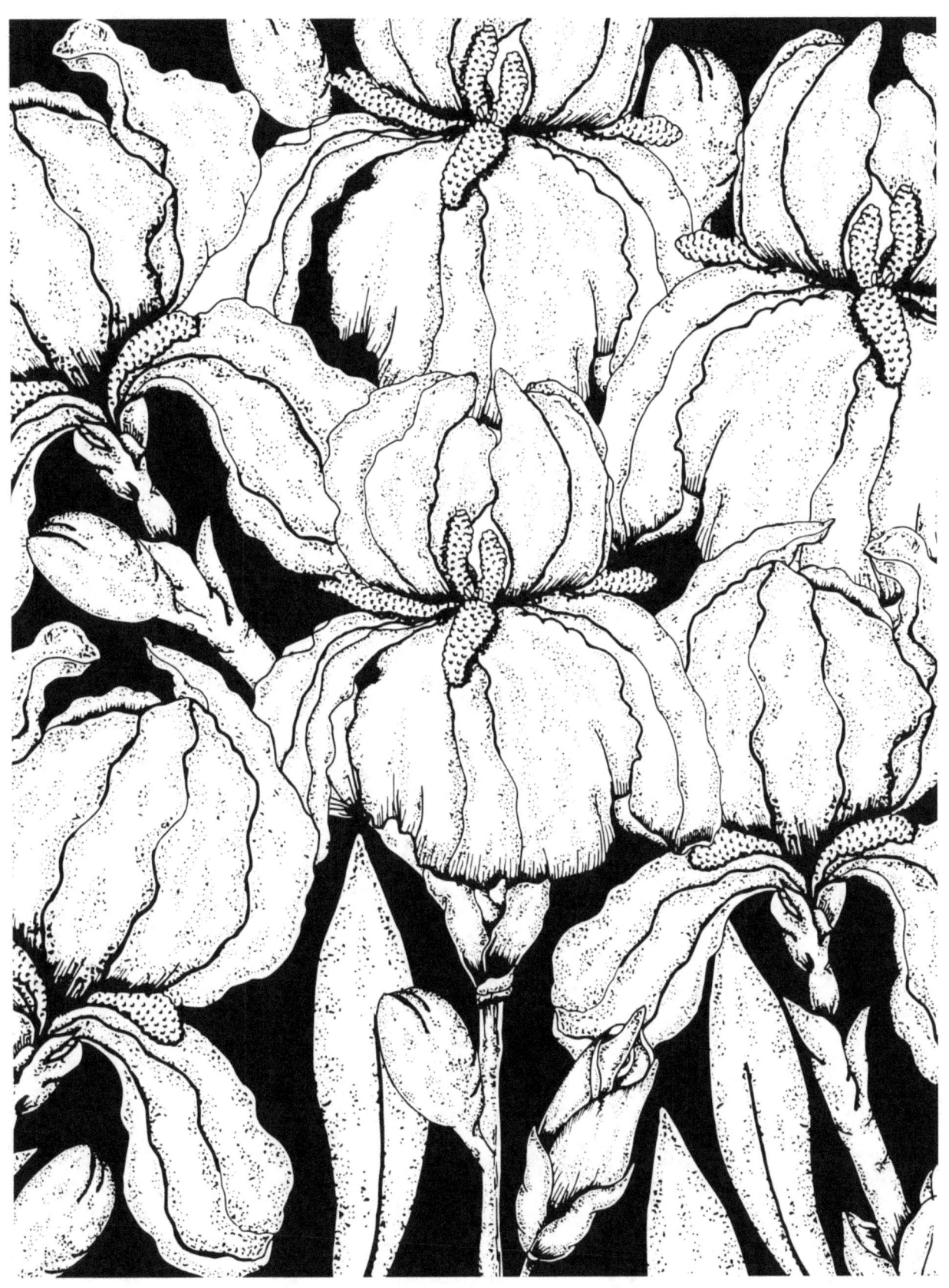

"There was cedar on the house within, carved in the shape of gourds and open flowers; all was cedar, there was no stone seen." (1 Kings 6:18)

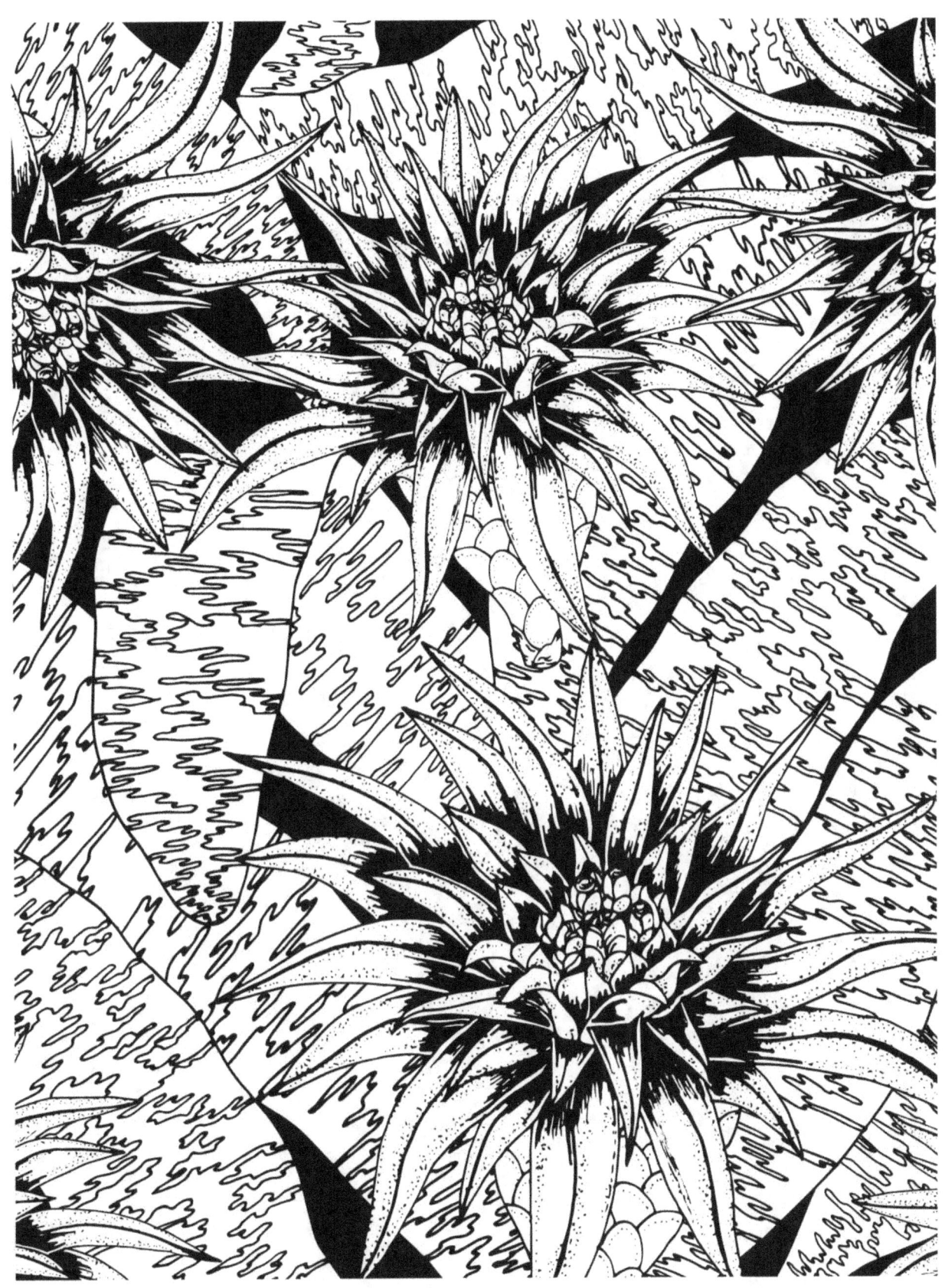

"Then he carved all the walls of the house roundabout with carved engravings of cherubim, palm trees, and open flowers, inner and outer sanctuaries." (1 Kings 6:29)

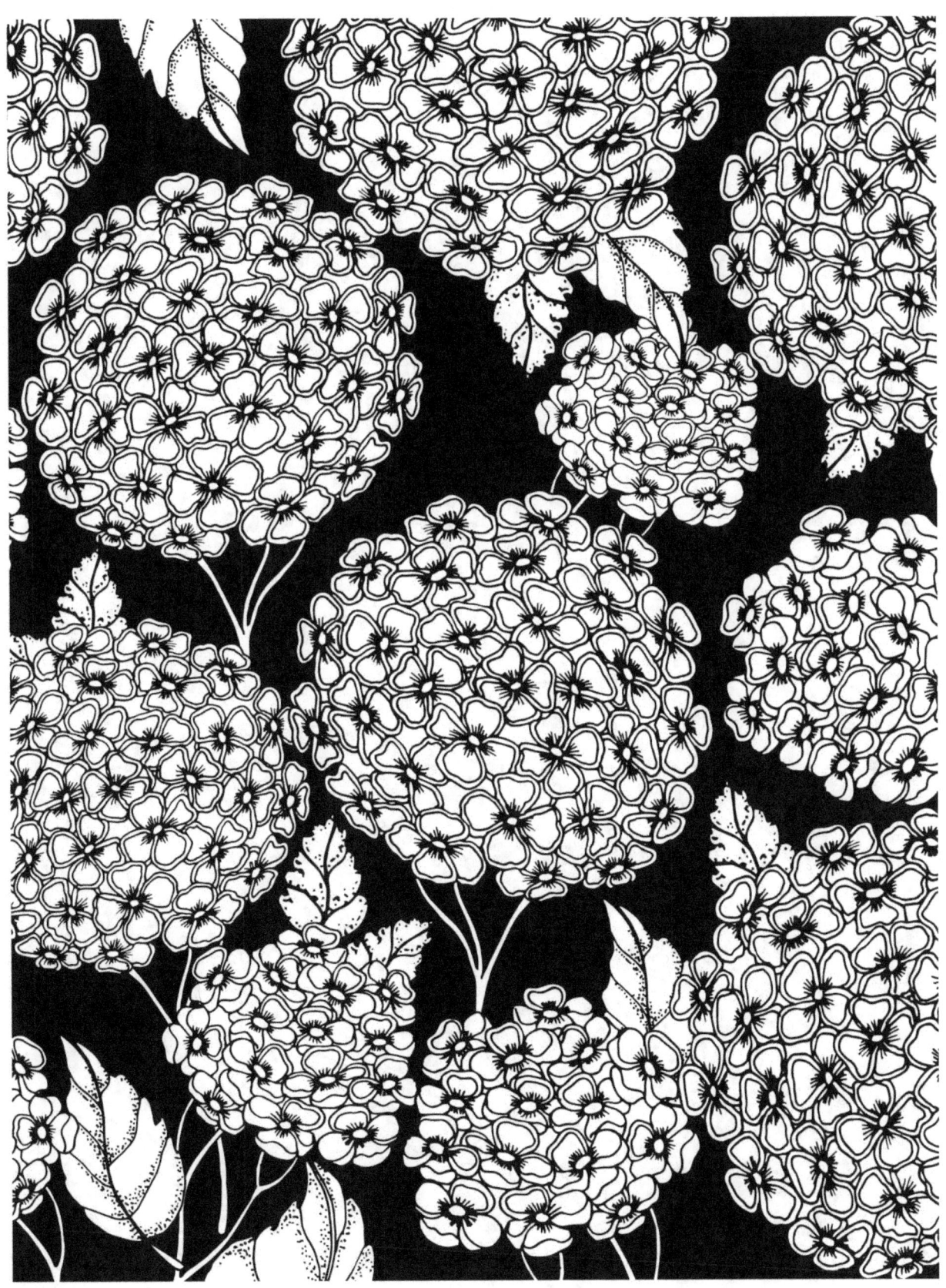

"The earth brought forth vegetation, plants yielding seed after their kind, and trees bearing fruit with seed in them, after their kind; and God saw that it was good."
(Genesis 1:12)

About The Author

Twylia Reid is a Best-Selling-Multi-Award-Winning Author and Multi-Published non-fiction writer. Her work has appeared in numerous publications, in print, and online. 2020 Success Women National Top Influencer Nominee, 2019 Trinity Nonprofit Awards Finalist, 2019 Blacks In Government Featured Speaker, 2019 110th NAACP Conference Featured Author/Panelist Moderator, 2019 Unspoken Wounds Women Veteran's Portrait of Personal Courage Award Recipient, 2019 ACHI (Strength In Sisterhood) Magazine Woman of Achievement & Author of the Year Award Nominee, 2018 48th Congressional Legislative Caucus Featured Author, 2019 Winner of The Authors Show Health/Fitness/Wellness Top Female Author, 2018 Winner of The Authors Show Female Non-Fiction Author, The Huffington Post Expert Feature Series "Who's Who –10 Black Female Experts to Watch in 2018" selected, and 2017 American Book Fest Best Book Awards Finalist.

Minister, speaker, entrepreneur, brain-injury-community advocate and caregiver, she's the Founder of Broken Wings, Inc., a 501(c)3 non-profit organization created to assist brain injury survivors and their families, Founder of When Heaven Speaks, LLC book coaching & publishing, Founder of Broken Wings Brain Injury Empowerment Group, Warring Women Arise and Pray Group, and the Executive Producer/Host of the Conquerors Café radio show where her knowledge and expertise is used as a conduit to help empower, educate, and enlighten survivors & caregivers of traumatic events by teaching them how to create the life they desire in spite of the challenges faced after a tragedy.

Her mantra is "Aspiring to Inspire Others!" To learn more, visit her website at www.twyliareid.com.

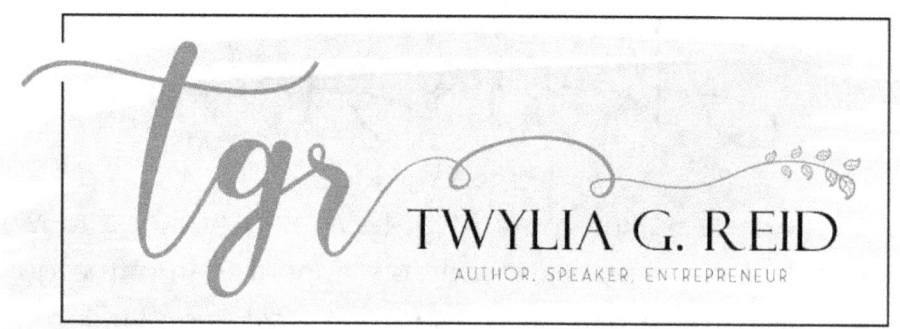

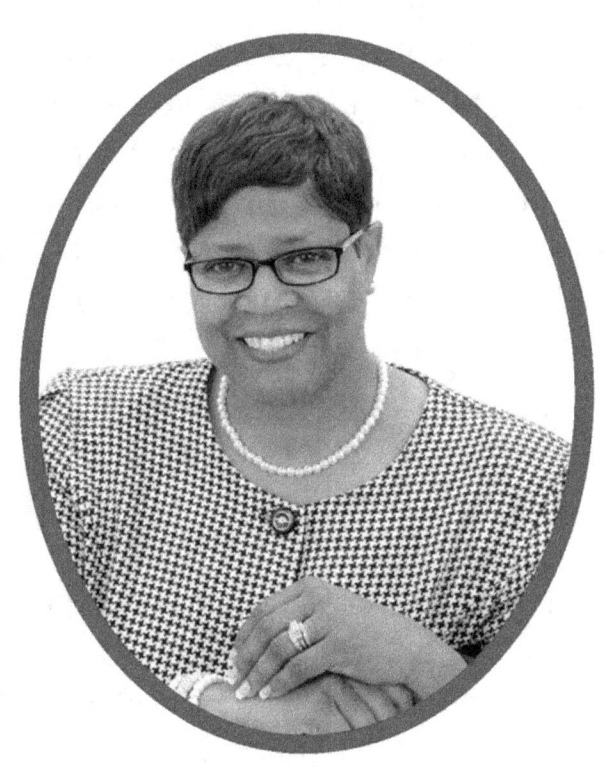

www.TwyliaReid.com
www.whenheavenspeakspublishing.com
www.brokenwingsinc.org

RECOMMENDED READINGS

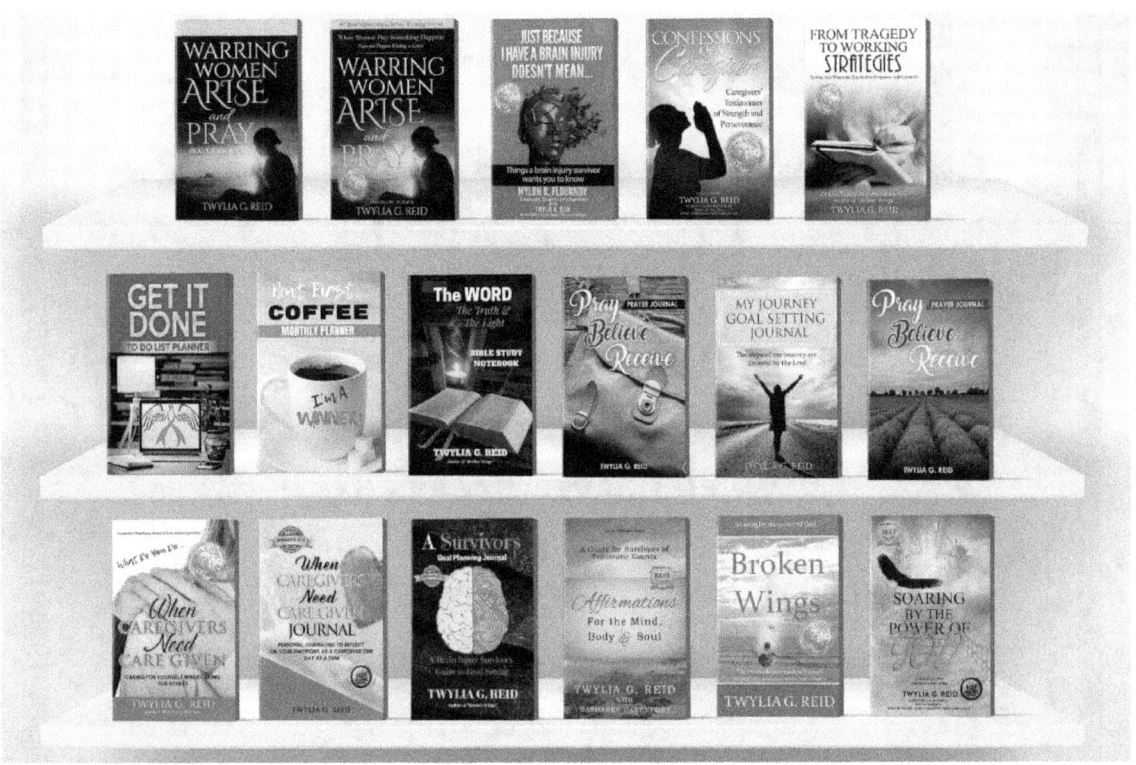

All books can be purchased from my website at
www.TwyliaReid.com
or
www.amazon.com/author/twyliareid

I pray this book is uplifting to your soul as you find peace and tranquility in the images on each page.

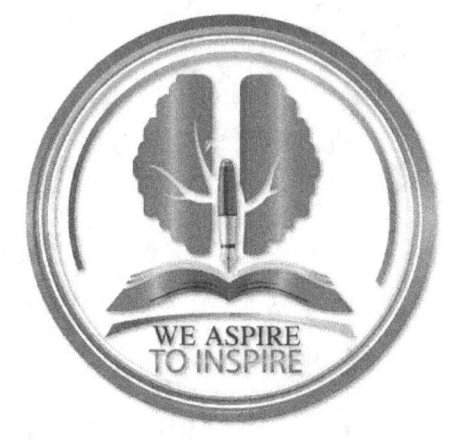

WHEN HEAVEN SPEAKS, LLC

www.whenheavenspeakspublishing.com

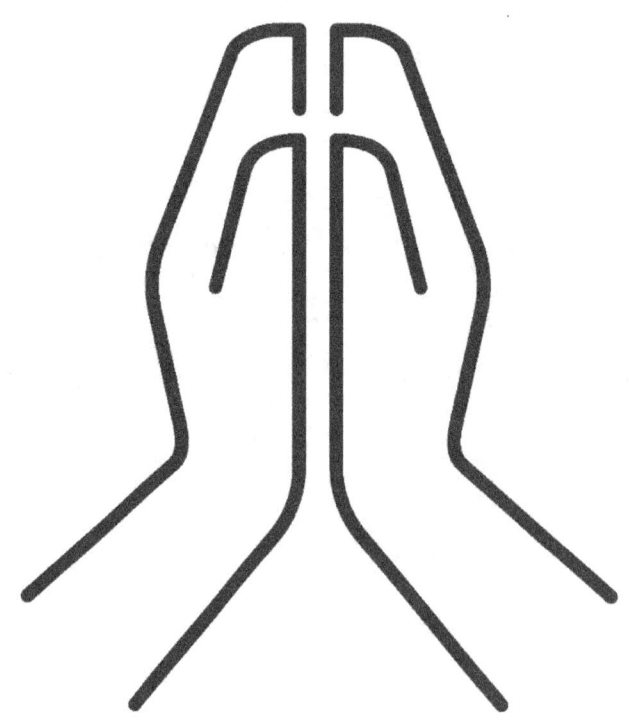

www.ingramcontent.com/pod-product-compliance
Lightning Source LLC
Chambersburg PA
CBHW081437220526
45466CB00008B/2426